YOUR CREATIVE WORK SPACE

THE SWEET SPOT STYLE GUIDE TO HOME OFFICE + STUDIO DECOR

desha peacock

Skyhorse Publishing

Skyhorse Publishing books may be purchased in bulk at special discounts for sales promotion, corporate gifts, fund-raising, or educational purposes. Special editions can also be created to specifications. For details, contact the Special Sales Department, Skyhorse Publishing, 307 West 36th Street, 11th Floor, New York, NY 10018 or info@skyhorsepublishing.com.

Skyhorse® and Skyhorse Publishing® are registered trademarks of Skyhorse Publishing, Inc.®, a Delaware corporation.

Visit our website at www.skyhorsepublishing.com.

10 9 8 7 6 5 4 3 2

Library of Congress Cataloging-in-Publication Data

Names: Peacock, Desha, author.
Title: Your creative work space : the sweet spot style guide to home office + studio decor / Desha Peacock.
Description: New York : Skyhorse Publishing, [2021] | Summary: "Design the ideal home office to fit your space, your personality, your work, and your dreams!"--Provided by publisher.
Identifiers: LCCN 2021018320 (print) | LCCN 2021018321 (ebook) | ISBN 9781510764590 (trade paperback) | ISBN 9781510712997 (epub)
Subjects: LCSH: Office decoration. | Home offices. | Interior decoration--Psychological aspects.
Classification: LCC NK2195.O4 P43 2021 (print) | LCC NK2195.O4 (ebook) | DDC 747.7--dc23
LC record available at https://lccn.loc.gov/2021018320
LC ebook record available at https://lccn.loc.gov/2021018321

Cover design by David Ter-Avanesyan
Front cover photo by Jo Chattman
Front cover photo styling by Alexandra Fraser—A V Studio & Co.
Back cover photo by Jo Chattman

Paperback ISBN: 978-1-5107-6459-0
Hardcover ISBN: 978-1-5107-1298-0
Ebook ISBN: 978-1-5107-1299-7

Printed in China

To Iyla,
keep pursuing your dreams and living in your sweet spot

contents

Detail of photographer Jo Chattman's studio.

introduction

Where you create.

We are all born with an innate desire to creatively express the essence of who we are. This desire is embedded into our soul, a gift at birth, our own Northern Star in a galaxy full of the unknown. It's the one true thing we know that we'll always have, regardless of the circumstances that surround us.

For most of us, that core desire has been nearly lost many times. It's been laughed at, degraded, humbled, and, for some, it's been simply pushed aside and forgotten. But don't worry, it's still there. More than that, it wants to be acknowledged. It wants to be heard, seen, and shared. It wants to be expressed.

You might think it was abandoned forever, hidden under a veil, but in truth it will surface whether you call it out or not. If unattended, it will seep out in the form of misplaced ambition, anger, depression, or resentment, or it may just present itself in a cloud of mild melancholy.

But it's still there.

It's the thing we are all born with. It's the reason you are here. It might be one thing or many things. It may come to you with force or barely show itself under the mist. But it's there and it wants your attention.

You may call it your work. You may call it your purpose. Maybe it's your calling. Whatever the name, it doesn't matter. You know what I'm talking about. It's who you are and why you are here.

This book is an offering that you might acknowledge the importance of your work, call it into being, and create a sacred nest in which it can be held and grow.

Your Creative Work Space

It's funny, because when I was approached to write a book on home office decor, I was super pumped because I love combining the theme of work with decor. It unites everything I've been working on for the last few years. But to be completely honest, I am not a big fan of the word *office*.

Office implies work. Work has its own negative connotations: *I have to go to work* sounds like a duty. It often *is* a duty, something we *have* to do. For most, there's a gentle aching around this word. For others, it's full-on drudgery.

Certainly, there may be times when we have to do things we don't want to do, but, overall, work should not feel like drudgery. After all, we spend most of our lives doing it. What would it be like if instead of dreading it, you ached for it? What if, instead of feeling depleted, you felt energized by it? What if you could not wait to get to it?

If you are doing creative work that you love now, congratulations, you are part of a small army of very lucky folk. If that's not the case, I implore you to consider doing *something* that brings you joy, if not an all-encompassing fever.

So, this thing, this passion, this drive that lights you up, let's call that your **creative work**. This creative work lives inside you. It can be harbored or unleashed at any time through any means. The utter truth is that you can have access to this creative juice without any outside influence. However, there are certain things that can help call it out. The two most important factors to opening up channels for your creative work to flow through you are your mental space and your physical space.

One can greatly influence the other. In this book, we are going to primarily focus on how your physical space can enhance your creative work flow.

In **Your Sacred Nest**, you'll learn why everyone needs a creative sweet spot work space, as well as how to discover what the sweet spot means to you.

We'll also discuss **The Evolution of the Creative Work Space** and how technology has changed how and where we work. Hello *freedom*!

I used to be sure that a clear space indicated a clear mind, but I've come to learn that some people (particularly artists!) really do thrive in a wee bit of *chaos*. No judgment. What's important is knowing what your preferred work style is.

I'll also share my own personal creative work spaces—yes, I have more than one!

Beyond my personal creative spaces, I'd like to share stories of creatives who have taken the time to thoughtfully create a beautiful work space that helps truly inspire them to do the work they are meant to do. We'll talk to artists, writers, bloggers, stylists, designers, and decorators, some of whom work from

Artist Johanna Starks in her home office in Sweden.

home and others who have 9–5 jobs. We'll also talk to **Gypsetters**, those who roam from place to place doing work they love in a truly *virtual office*.

From their stories, I hope that you will feel inspired to not only create an amazing work space, but also to take action to move forward with your own creative ambitions and dreams.

Shall we?

Your Sacred Nest: Everyone Needs a Creative Sweet Spot Space

Whether it's an entire studio with a view or a little nook in your living room, we all deserve a little space of our own. Just like a nest built by a mother bird for her chicks, it's not really the size that matters, but the love that's put into creating a space that serves its purpose. A mother bird doesn't complain that she doesn't have the time or space to create her nest, she just makes do with the resources available to her at the time. She gets creative, because she knows time is of the essence.

Her job isn't finished when the nest is built. She still needs to protect it until her babies are strong enough to go out on their own.

Just like the momma bird making a nest, you also need to put some time and thought into creating your space, but don't get too caught up in the details. Think of what would happen if the momma bird neglected to actually build the nest because she couldn't find the perfect materials. Don't let your creativity suffer or, worse, *die* because you can't find the perfect lamp or Berber rug. In other words, don't worry if it's not perfect. Use the resources you have around you and allow them to blossom with age and use.

Once you create your space, do not abandon it. Protect it fiercely with that momma bird love. Make a plan to spend time there until your creative projects are finished and ready to be set free into the world to be appreciated.

Considering that I have several creative work spaces in my house, it's not so much about making one sacred space, but making my work within whatever space I'm in, sacred. For example, if I'm working in my bedroom office, I have a ritual of opening the curtains, cleaning my desk, having a cup of tea or water by my side, and diffusing essential oils that uplift and energize.

Sweet Spot Style Tip

Use essential oils in your creative work space to . . .

1. **Gain focus and clarity:** frankincense, lime, ylang-ylang, Hawaiian sandalwood

2. **Combat fatigue:** peppermint, white fir, lemon, basil, thyme, rosemary, orange, lemongrass, eucalyptus

3. **Invite calm:** lavender, roman chamomile, ylang-ylang, cedarwood, myrrh, juniper berry, rose, geranium, bergamot

In the summer, I often work on my front porch. My rituals are slightly different there. No need to open any curtains because the light pours in from all directions. I still have my cup of tea or water nearby. Instead of the diffuser, I might choose incense, such as Copal or Palo Santo.

When I'm working, I need to focus. So before I prepare my space and sit down to work, I ask my family to refrain from interrupting me. I often turn my cell phone to silent, and sometimes I set a timer to help me focus on one task at a time.

These rituals help create a sacred space that says: *this work is important and valuable to me.*

What kind of nest are you building?

Are you putting enough love into your nest, while at the same time allowing it to emerge with the resources that you have on hand?

What rituals can you implement to create a sacred space within your home or office?

What distractions can you let go of so you can turn your full attention to your creative work?

If you have others in or around your space, how do they know that you are in *do not disturb* mode?

Supplies for creating a sacred nest and pretty creative work space.
Always start with a clean work space with good lighting, then add . . .

1 **Candles**

2 **Incense** (try Copal or Palo Santo)

3 **Essential oils and diffuser** (try frankincense or lavender)

4 **Music**

5 **Tea and water**

6 **Fresh flowers**

After surveying my followers on social media, I discovered that one of the biggest challenges you all have is organization. Paper and paperwork is a big problem! Here are some tips to help you clear away that paper clutter.

Let's talk about the mail

Oy vey. We get lots of mail, don't we? You need a system for dealing with all the paper that comes through the mail. I use the *Stop It in Its Tracks* system. *Do not* put the mail on your dining room table or in a stack on your desk. NO! When the mail comes, it goes from the mailbox directly to the recycle bin or the bill container.

The bill container should be close to where you would normally set the mail upon entering your home. My bill container is an organizational system with a chalkboard and two slots. One slot is for the bills. The second slot is for my husband that contains gift cards, etc.

Other stuff that comes in the mail and what to do with it:

- Most cards get read and recycled. Special cards, like handwritten thank-you cards, go into a slot in the back of my vision book.

- Birthday invitations go into the calendar and then get recycled.

- Coupons get recycled at my house; if you use coupons, put those in a separate place, like near your shopping bags or in a special pocket of your wallet.

BILLS—All your bills should go in one place. Pick one day a week to pay your bills. Once a bill is paid, the rest of the paperwork that goes with that bill gets recycled. Document when you paid the bill and the check number, so if there's a problem you will have that information available. Even better, pay your bills online.

TAXES—You need to keep the last seven years of your tax records. Many people keep their tax records in a file cabinet. It doesn't have to be ugly. There are lots of cool vintage/industrial file cabinets out there for any budget. Every year after you file your taxes, you can destroy a file that goes back eight years. This way you'll only have seven years of taxes stored.

Sweet Spot Style Tip

Avoid cord clutter. A mound of electrical cords will detract from your pretty sweet spot space. My solution is this little cabinet that I bought for about $10 second hand and painted creamy peach. Behind these sliding doors is all my ugly stuff. My router, phone cords, and printer cables all live there. Here's how to make your own.

1   **Make a 4-inch hole in the back** of your cabinet using a hand saw or reciprocating saw. If you have a hole saw bit that fits onto an electric drill, that will make a nice, clean hole.

2   **Place your electronics inside the cabinet.**

3   **Thread the cords out the hole** in the back, then plug them in. It's just that easy.

MAGAZINES + NEWSPAPERS—Does anyone still read newspapers? If you do, this is an easy one. Just recycle it after you've read it. If you haven't read it by the time the next paper arrives, don't fool yourself into thinking you'll read it later. Just let it go. I love magazines, and boy do they build up fast. I have a hard time recycling those, so if I have time, I'll pull my favorite photos out and put them in my folder in my vision book, where I'll paste them later. For recipes, pull those out and put them into a menu book or recipe folder. If I haven't pulled my favorite photos, articles, or recipes out after one year, then the whole thing gets recycled.

CHILDREN'S ART—If you're reading this book, I assume that you are creative. If you have kids, it's probably important to you that your child has every opportunity to create. The only problem is kids generate *lots* of art! What do you do with it all?

My system: I don't skimp on encouraging my daughter to create, *ever*. From the time she was old enough to draw she had markers, paints, glitter, glue, sequins, feathers . . . the whole nine yards. My girl produced.

Seriously, if I were to keep everything my daughter made, we would not have room in our house to sit, eat, or sleep. It would be one big house full of art! Every mother feels bad throwing away our babe's art, but it needs to be done. Here's how do it:

Age 1-3: Collect all the art in one big pile. Take the best and put it in an artist portfolio.

After age 3: Collect all the art in one big pile. Sit on the floor with your child and ask them to separate the piles into two categories: keep and recycle. They get to have control over what they keep and learn to discern the good from the not so good. This is a great lesson for your kiddos, so that as they get older they can do this with their clothes, toys, and so on.

Please note, getting rid of art that you just made, whether as a child or an adult, is hard. The more time that goes by, the less precious it will feel and your child will be able to lessen the grip and let go of more. My daughter is ten, and we have large art binders for every year of her life, but that's still a lot.

Now we can go back and start consolidating those folders. Since she's now in fourth grade, letting go of what she made in preschool is way easier than letting go of the paper tree houses she made last week. Basically, you are narrowing it down, so that each year the art is whittled down to the best pieces, a visual timeline of your little artist's creative growth.

Your Child's Sacred Nest

Everyone in your family needs a place to call their own, even if it's just a little nook. I often find that when I create a new sweet spot nook for myself, my daughter often wants to take over. When that happens, I have to remember that she craves the same thing I do: a pretty place to play or dream.

So, instead of shunning her (well, sometimes I have to if I'm in the middle of work), I try to help her create a space of her own. When your child, or partner for that matter, has their own sweet spot space, they won't feel compelled to enter yours. Everyone deserves to have a little corner (or more!) where they can truly feel at home. (See For Tots and Teens, page 221, for more tips on how to help create a sweet spot space for your child.)

What Is the Sweet Spot?

The sweet spot is the intersection of all that's good. It is self-defined depending on what *good* means to you.

On a spiritual level, being in my sweet spot means doing work that is creative, fulfilling, meaningful, and fun while making a fantastic living.

The longer version is that I have a strong desire to live up to my full potential. I am ambitious in living out my purpose. I am enamored by beauty and want to be surrounded by it. My intention is to create a beautiful and financially abundant life*style* for me and my family that consists of the creative work that I am meant to do.

On a physical level. I like to be surrounded by beauty. It inspires me. My intention is to have a lovely home and several creative work spaces that light me up and energize me.

At home, I have several sweet spot spaces that I create from. I recently remodeled my bedroom, and I love to work from there. It's mostly white with one wall of floral wallpaper. My simple white desk is from Ikea, and the pink velvet chair was a tag sale purchase for $10. I literally rolled it down the street to my house one summer day. I like to work from this office setup in my bedroom because the white walls calm me and allow me to focus, while the rest of the room feels feminine with a touch of bohemian charm that speaks to me.

In the summer, I also spend a lot of time working from my front porch. The Internet is good there. There's a table, a chair, and a beautiful view of my garden. It's quiet, and I like to be outside as much as possible. The fresh air is energizing.

It's really important for everyone to have his or her own space to create, but your space might not look anything like mine.

Your turn. Tell me, what kind of space delights you on both a spiritual and physical level? What does your sweet spot space look like? How does it make you feel?

A peek into the author's bedroom work space

The Evolution of the Creative Work Space

While the majority of employed people still work 9–5, there is a work revolution happening that is shifting the way we work and the way we think about work. Whereas entrepreneurs have always had the luxury of setting their own hours, the Internet is allowing us to work from virtually anywhere.

Whether you are an entrepreneur or not, most people have a home office or at least a place where they file important papers and pay the bills. Yet, for most of us, we don't necessarily need the traditional home office anymore. As long as we have our laptop and cell phone, we can just as easily work from a café. In fact, I'm working from the history room in my local library right now because it's quiet and there are no distractions.

As the virtual world evolves, so will the way we work. Right now we struggle with paper and cord clutter, but soon more devices will be cordless. People already read books on their devices and pay bills online. As new technology emerges, the need for a home office might become obsolete. Yet, some things will always remain steady. An artist will always need space for canvases and paints. Most creators will always prefer natural light.

Sarah Bennett's Top 10 Feng Shui Tips for the Creative Work Space

Without a doubt, our environment influences our body, mind, and spirit. In this day and age, many of us spend much of our time sitting at a desk in our designated work space. It's not the best for our health, but there are ways to liven up your space and make it work for you, not against you. We can do this through mindful arrangement, otherwise known as the art of feng shui.

Feng shui is a practice that offers guidance in arranging our space. There are different schools of thought within feng shui practices. However, the overarching idea is that arranging our physical objects in certain ways can affect the flow of energy, thus improving our lives. When chi (or energy) can flow easily, our space will lift us up and positively support us.

I've gathered my top ten favorite feng shui tips to help you design your optimal creative work space.

1. Tidy up and organize. Clutter brings energy down and overwhelms us. Take time to sift through all your clutter and clear your space. It's suggested that you carve out specific times during the week to tidy up and get organized. Better yet, make tidying up part of your morning ritual. Even if it's just ten minutes to clear your desk area or clean up your computer desktop.

It's also a good idea to clean and organize on a deeper level at the end of each season. Clear out the cobwebs and make room for new ideas. Ask yourself if each item in your work area is serving a purpose for you. Is it providing a physical purpose for your work? Does it still bring you joy? If not, let it go!

Use a Bagua map when deciding where to place items on your desktop.

Ultimately, setting aside time to deep clean your work space will bring in fresh new energy, increase motivation, and invite productive energy. One last thing to keep in mind is to make sure everything in your work space has a place. This goes for *everything*: pens, pencils, papers, books, paints, paintbrushes, etc.; make a place for each item. Every item deserves a home.

2. Position your desk. The desk position is a biggie. Ideally, you want to be farther away from the door and positioned in a way so your back does not face the door. In feng shui this is called the commanding position. By facing the open doorway, you are inviting success and business. If you're unable to move your desk in this position, bring in a mirror so you can see a reflection of the door. Your desk should draw you in and excite you; keep this in mind when placing it.

3. Lighting. Natural light is always the best. If you are lucky to have windows, there's no need to decorate with curtains; bare windows will allow for optimal light. If you do have curtains, make sure to pull them back to allow as much light flow as possible. Fluorescent lights are a no-no. If you need more light, just bring in a few lamps. A desk lamp will help with focus and efficiency, and a larger lamp will create a better ambiance for your work space.

4. Greenery. You can never have too many plants! Plants help increase oxygen in our environment, which is a big help when you're working indoors. Bringing in at least one large plant is ideal. Electronics release EMFs (electromagnetic fields) that are harmful to our health over time. Plants help absorb some of those toxins. Look for any air-purifying plants, such as ferns, palms, or the classic money tree. Just make sure you tend to your plants. Find pretty pots that you are drawn to in different textures and colors. Anything goes, as long as it's visually appealing to you.

5. Desktop arrangement. At least 50 percent of your desktop should be clear at all times. There are specific areas on your desk that can assist in your success. A Bagua map is a wonderful grid that helps with arrangement; use this as your guide (see the diagram on page XXI for a visual). Think about the areas in your life where you'd like to see improvement. For wealth and prosperity, focus on the back left corner of the desk by placing a plant, crystal, or even your computer in this spot. Career is front and center. You'll want to keep this spot clear but can include affirmations and motivational quotes to glance at.

6. Less is more. Make sure you are picky with what furniture you bring into your work space. Too much furniture blocks chi flow and can create chaos and blockage. For a healthy setup, stick with the *less is more* rule.

7. The chair. Your desk chair is very important. This is what supports you in your everyday work. You'll want to make sure your chair has good back support. If you have a pretty chair that doesn't provide support, this can lead to stress and strain. The best solution is to find a chair that is visually exciting for you that also physically supports your body and makes you feel comfortable.

When using lots of color, keep your palette clean with a white wall, as seen at the Jungalow Headquarters, where Justina Blakeney and her team create magic.

8. Crystalize. A jade cicada is helpful for keeping confrontations away. It also brings in good luck!

9. Color. Based on your style, color is a personal preference. To help find a color that supports you, take a look at the Bagua map of your creative space and reference the feng shui color wheel. Above all, ask yourself how the color makes you feel. Our instincts are our best compass in choosing colors. Don't be afraid to play. It might take a few tries to figure out what color story works best for you. A good tip is to try color in small bursts through artwork or textiles first before painting an entire room.

10. Have fun. In the end, the most important thing is to have fun. Instead of incorporating these tips as a *job*, approach it in a playful way. It's your space to be productive, after all, so claim it as your own and let it reflect *you*! When you walk into your work space you want to feel welcomed and inspired to do the work you are meant to do.

Read more about Sarah's work and her design style on page 151.

Choose the Right Light

Lighting is a big deal. It can make or break a space. Worse, if we have the wrong lighting installed, such as fluorescents, it may lead to problems like migraines, eye strain, mood swings, lack of productivity, and mental blockages.

Natural light is always best. Nothing is better than a big window or French doors to let the light pour in and make your day sunny and bright. If you aren't blessed with loads of natural light, you'll need another source. Overhead lighting tends to be harsh. Lamps, wall sconces, and task lighting are generally a better choice.

Etsy shop owner Sarah Bennett keeps a Himalayan salt lamp on her desk to help neutralize the negative effects of electronics.

A tip to **brighten a dark space** is to add a mirror. Mirrors reflect light and can brighten a space if placed near light.

Here are a few tips to keep in mind when searching for sufficient lighting:

1. **A 6500K lightbulb** is comparable to daylight. If this doesn't work for you, find a softer neutral white lightbulb around 4100K. A cooler white light boosts serotonin and helps us stay focused.

2. **It's recommended to have at least two light sources** in your work area. A larger overhead light and task lighting closer to where you are actually working.

3. **Halogen bulbs** work great for up close work.

4. **Try out an LED desk light.** This is great for task lighting, and you can change the color temps to see what works best for you.

5. **Himalayan salt lamps** are wonderful eco-friendly light sources that can help offset the massive amount of blue light we take in through electronic devices. They offer a warm glow that helps with mood and focus.

6. **Invest in mood-lifting lights.** Many of us have a hard time with the transition into winter due to the reduction in daylight hours. The effect can be magnified in regions with colder temperatures.

To reduce these effects, take a look at the Philips Wake-Up Light with Sunrise Simulation. Another product on the market is C by GE smart bulbs. This particular bulb can be adjusted to various color temps that help with your body's circadian rhythm. There is also an app that you can use to create a lighting schedule for yourself. Who knew lighting had gotten so fancy?

the salon

Create Your Sweet Spot Writing Space

As a writer, I know it can be hard to sit down and do the work. It seems many writers spend more time procrastinating about the work than actually doing it, myself included.

Unlike some types of artists, as a writer, you don't typically need a myriad of supplies to do your work. When your laptop is your primary tool, you are not restricted to one particular place to work. You can create your sweet spot writing place just about anywhere.

Whether you are writing from home or away from home, I've learned that most writers tend to do better when they have rituals.

Writing Outside the Home

Although I love working from home, when it comes to writing books, I prefer a change of scenery. Maybe it's because there are fewer distractions outside my home. I find it nearly impossible to write when my family is home. Maybe it's because I need that shift in physical space to put me in the mind-set of writing.

Whatever it is, my preference is to grab my laptop and hit the local café. Within easy reach is one hot cup of chai, water, and my pretty rose gold cell phone. Lately I've found that using the timer on my phone really helps me stay focused on one task at a time. Try setting your timer for forty-five-minute blocks. Then you can continue for another forty-five minutes or change tasks.

Every writer deserves an inspired place to create. At left is a sneak peek into where writer and interior designer Michelle Gage works her magic.

If you have a hard time focusing, get out of the house. Grab your laptop or journal and hit your local café or library. Changing your physical location can often help you get into that focused writing groove.

My Writing Rituals at Home

Today my family is out of the house for the entire day, so I'm currently writing from my home office. I love my home office because it's pretty, but it's easy to get distracted. To help me focus, I have a few no-fail rituals that help me prepare for writing.

Here's what I do to prepare me for a day of writing at home:

- First, I take a hot bath with lavender sea salts to help me relax.

- Next, I get dressed in a cute outfit. No one is home to see me, but looking good makes me feel good. It's also a preventive. If I stayed in my pj's all day, I would feel like a slouch, and if my writing was not inspired, I might look at myself and confirm that yes, I am a slouch. Basically, creating a beautiful work environment is the same as my personal style, both reflect who I am, and both need to attract positive and inspired energy. Thus, I get dressed!

- Then, I clean my desk. This is imperative. I have a soft white light for my work space. By my side is a glass of water and flowers. Living things give energy. I also use the power of aromatherapy and essential oils. I use a diffuser with frankincense for mental clarity and lavender for calmness.

- The ringer of my phone is off, and, once again, I have my timer by my side. Be sure to stand up and stretch or move about for a few minutes between each timed interval. This will help with fatigue so you can actually work longer.

Sweet Spot Style Tips for Writing at Home

1 **Start with a clean desk.**

2 **Add flowers** to inspire.

3 **Use a diffuser** with essential oils for focus.

4 Make sure to **have soft white light** to avoid eyestrain.

5 **Don't work in your yoga pants;** get dressed so you can feel confident in yourself and your work.

6 **Use a timer** to help you focus on one task at a time.

7 **Stand up every forty-five minutes** and stretch or walk around to reduce fatigue.

the stylist's studio

Create Your Sweet Spot Studio or Shop

As more and more women start businesses online, we are seeing a massive increase in very cool online shops. Smart lady bosses know that a beautiful online presence with gorgeously styled products leads to sales. In this section, you'll meet a mix of designers, stylists, online shop owners, bloggers, authors, and photographers with a focus on *style*!

A snapshot of photographer and stylist Jo Chattman's studio in Greenfield, Massachusetts.

Anna Louise Harris

I am: Vintage Shopkeeper, Tiny House Owner, Unrealistic Dreamer
My home: Portland, Oregon
My style: Simple. Earthy.

Everything about my work space reflects my core values, which is basically aspiring to live my dream lifestyle.

I first discovered Anna Louise on Instagram and fell in love with her unique style, which is a delicate balance of earthy vintage goodness. She runs a sweet online shop called *Experimental Vintage*, where you can find beautiful vintage textiles, rugs, and other home decor items and apparel.

Your Creative Work

I started selling vintage as a hobby after I lost my day job as a school counselor in California during the budget crisis in 2008. I was still working nights at the local French-American restaurant that had helped me pay my way through college, but all of a sudden I was working twenty-five hours a week instead of my usual sixty-plus.

I am a go-go-go type of person and became mildly depressed because of my sudden onset of free time. At the advice of a dear friend, I opened an Etsy shop. I still remember the very first item I sold, a funky 1970s carpet bag purse.

I was immediately hooked on the entire process of selling vintage, and this is when my shop *Experimental Vintage*

was born. Fast-forward eight years, and here I am, selling vintage full time and still absolutely loving it.

How does your current creative work space help you do the work you were meant to do?

I ran my business out of my home for the first seven years. As my business grew, it became clear that I needed a larger, separate work space. I have been in my studio for about a year now. It's the best investment I've made thus far for my business.

I searched high and low in Portland for a place that would first and foremost be a perfect photo studio. Since I sell online, a great product shot is just as important as the product itself. I ended up finding the perfect studio in a great part of inner North Portland. I'm on the second floor of a beautiful early-1900s building. My studio has white walls, tall ceilings, wood floors, and four big east-facing windows, which gives me perfect filtered light all day long.

In addition, it's large enough (roughly 400 square feet) for me to have a dedicated shipping area for packaging up orders. Having a simple, well-lit, blank space for me to do product photography has been a game changer. I've also been able to reclaim my guest bedroom at home, an added bonus!

Staying Organized

Every evening, as I lie in bed, I mentally plan out what my next day needs to look like. Every day is a little different for me, and sometimes I don't know what needs to happen until it's actually happening (e.g., there's a great estate sale happening on the other side of town and I need to drop what I'm doing and run over there), so having a preset game plan allows me to stay sane, even when it ends up that I can't follow it. Also, I've been working on streamlining and batching my work.

For me, this means simple things like taking all my product photography at one time, then doing all of my editing at another time, then listing products in my shop at a different time all at once. It's kind of hard for me to stick to that process, especially when I'm super excited about an item I've found for the shop (most likely a great rug!). My immediate urge is to photograph, edit, and list that one item. But I've noticed that by constantly switching gears, I'm losing a lot of time in the process. By completing my tasks in a bulk-like manner, I've cut my task transition time down immensely, which means more productivity in the long run.

Biggest Challenge

Initially, the biggest challenge about my creative work space was the cost that it added to my operational expenses. I ran *Experimental Vintage* out of my guest room and basement for the first seven years. Now, I feel so lucky to walk into this space every day, although it did take me a few months to grow my business to catch up with the extra cost. Taking the leap to invest in a studio space was a scary thing for me, but my business has since grown in ways that I'd never even imagined beforehand.

Pretty + Practical

With new inventory coming in daily, it can be a challenge for me to keep my work space organized and well merchandised for photographs. Twice a week, I set aside a small amount of time for a cleaning/revamp. I'll walk into my studio and spend twenty minutes tidying up and moving products and plants around so that they're always aesthetically pleasing to my eye.

I love how this process always keeps my work space looking and feeling fresh. Also, having a clean and organized studio makes me feel as though I have a blank space to create in. Ideas come to me more easily the less I'm surrounded by untidiness. It's the classic *clear space, clear mind* perspective, and it definitely applies to me and my personality type.

Sweet Spot Style Living

Working in my sweet spot means so many things to me. First of all, it reminds me that my business is always growing, a sort of personal validation.

Initially, I had a lot of anxiety when I chose to abandon the career path (that I spent eight years in college for) to pursue this passion of mine.

Having this space makes me feel successful in ways that I need to. Also, it has helped me to reclaim my home. I actually have a guest room now. It used to be my home office/shipping center/photography studio, etc. Walking into a clean home every day and having a dedicated space for friends and family to stay when they visit me in Portland has done so much to improve my mental psyche.

Core Values

Everything about my work space reflects my core values, which is basically aspiring to live my dream lifestyle. For me, this means indulging in the simple pleasures of life. I walk to work most days, a four-mile round trip. I get in my exercise, chat with neighbors who are working in their yards, smell flowers, and pick up feathers on my way.

Upon arriving, I usually treat myself to an Americano from my favorite coffee shop across the street. Then I head upstairs, crank up my music, and allow myself to be creative. I honestly love the whole process of staging and photographing items. It's my creative outlet, and I feel so lucky to be able to do it on a daily basis in such a beautiful and well-lit space.

Before the workday is over, I always head downstairs to chat with the shop owners below me. Making personal connections with other humans is so important to me, and having a space away from home where I can do this is invaluable. I also love having local clients stop by and getting the opportunity to meet them in person. I honestly love what I do for a living, and it feels so great to be able to share this excitement with my customers when I can.

Style Tips

Allow yourself to indulge in a few key items, like the perfect work desk or a great rug. I spent a little more than I'm usually comfortable with on the few furniture/textile items that are staples in my studio, but I honestly love them. They set the tone for the whole space.

Find Anna online at experimentalvintage.com and on Instagram @_annalouise and @experimentalvintage.

Holly Becker

I am: Author, Stylist, Journalist, Founder of decor8blog.com and bloggingyourway.com

My home: Germany

My style: Open. Quirky. Clear. Friendly. Inviting. Playful.

Visualize where you see yourself and believe you can get there no matter what.

Holly Becker is the creative mind behind the incredibly popular lifestyle and home interiors blog, decor8. She's also an international bestselling author of four books and has taught more than 8,000 students globally about blogging, social media, interior styling, and photography.

It was during one of Holly's first Blogging Your Way e-courses that I started to see how I could piece together my own creative career. I was working full time in academia at the time, but desperately wanted to expand into a creative career that was financially abundant, meaningful, and fun. I was inspired by Holly's story of how she created a business and lifestyle based on her passions. Taking her course opened my eyes to the endless possibilities of how to craft an online creative career.

Now, five years later, I'm a full-time entrepreneur doing work I love. I'm so deeply grateful that I found Holly when I did. I'd like to acknowledge the profound impact Holly and her work has had on my own creative career path. Thank you, Holly!

Your Creative Work

I was in design school after exiting the corporate world as a project manager, something I realized I wasn't interested in doing for the rest of my life. While in design school, I started to take clients, and they told me how they wish they could tap into my ideas day and night, and I thought about blogging because I had just started reading *Apartment Therapy*. It was a new blog, and I imagined being able to blog about design and decorating, too—why not? I thought I could eventually start writing about design for magazines too, so maybe a blog would give me some practice writing but also be a bit of a portfolio that I could point editors to, and also find new clients and satisfy current clients who wanted to tap into my brain for ideas and inspiration. It started primarily because I loved writing about design and sharing my favorite resources, and I really wanted to connect with people online who had similar interests.

Your Creative Work Space

It's sunny and has a beautiful view of the turn-of-the-century buildings across the street; I find the view and the sunshine very motivating. I also like the peaceful feeling I have working from home—my neighbors are gone all day, so it's completely silent. As a writer, the silence is wonderful. Yet I don't feel isolated because my desk overlooks the city view, so I still feel like I'm around people all day even though I'm not. (My assistant lives in Malta, so, sadly, I never see her.) I also love the big room I have to work in; I feel honored to be able to work in such a beautiful room in my home that is dedicated to my work.

I started my blog working from a three-room, 1875 carriage house in New Hampshire back in 2006. My desk was near my bed, so I've definitely come a long way since then. My dream to live abroad and to have such a nice work studio wasn't an easy road, but I'm so glad I stuck with my dreams and went for it. My work space is a daily reminder of how far dedication and a positive outlook can get you.

Staying On Task

My work is flexible. I stay on task because I set deadlines that are reasonable and I work when I can, around my son's schedule and moods.

Toddlers are so unpredictable! I know I have to work six days a week, but Saturday is only a few hours, and during the week my husband takes our boy in the morning and I have him mainly in the afternoons. At night, I work after he goes to bed until 11:00 p.m. or midnight. I work less than I did before having a child, but I'm twice as productive because I know my time is so limited. Limitations definitely make you more creative!

Biggest Challenge

I wish I could host workshops in this space. I did, about five years ago, and it was wonderful, but, I must confess, having fifteen to twenty people in your home for a workshop can feel too close for comfort. I loved and never regretted the workshop I hosted back then, but I knew I'd never do it again in my private home. Eventually, I will take a work space outside of my home for this purpose.

I also would rather *not* work from home once my son gets older and is in school because I want him to freely come and go as he pleases after school without me always complaining to him to be quiet or not bother me or my clients. I want to eventually keep family life and work life very separate so I also can "shut off" at home and not always have the business on my mind because it's in the other room.

Pretty + Practical

Storage—my desk is an IKEA hack using cabinets, wheels as legs, and a custom top I had made to fit. It holds everything and was relatively affordable.

I also have a large white wooden cabinet with solid doors where I hide all of my arts and crafts supplies. My bookcase is another great place to store things, mostly books. Then I have another cabinet in the room with doors where I store all of my camera equipment and tech gear. When everything has a place, cleanup is a breeze, and keeping things organized isn't a problem.

Sweet Spot Style Living

While my son is young and not in school yet, it means I get to be with this wonderful little boy each day and never miss a single moment of his growth, curiosity, and craziness. It's my sweet spot because I get to enjoy my two favorite things, my family and my work, each day. Even though it can be hard and exhausting at times, I feel really honored to get the best of both worlds like this. I really mean it. As much as it drives me crazy some days, I wouldn't have it any other way.

Core Values

My belief is that family is of fundamental importance *and* that women should never take the back seat—that a woman *can* have a family *and* a career and do both really well, not perfect, but really well. Having my work space at home currently gives me the chance to put my family first and my job in close second, so I feel like I'm fulfilled as a mother and as a very driven working woman. I don't feel like I had to give up something I love in order to have a family.

Style Tips

My original sweet spot, when I launched my blog, was in the corner of my bedroom near the bed. I bought a desk from West Elm, my first Mac, and have never looked back! I didn't have the perfect work environment crammed into my little room that I shared with my husband, but I definitely had the drive and passion, and I believed that one day the dedication would somehow pay off. I remember telling my husband over a decade ago that I always envisioned living abroad in Europe, being a writer for a living, writing my books near the window overlooking a beautiful European street with historic buildings. I've since relocated to northern Germany and have the exact spot near the window overlooking a city with pretty buildings I had imagined.

I guess my biggest tip is to visualize where you see yourself and believe you can get there no matter what. And please don't wait for circumstances to be right or perfect—just get started; taking a little step each day in the right direction is definitely going to get you closer to your sweet spot. Always believe in that truth!

Find Holly online at decor8blog.com, bloggingyourway.com, and on Instagram @decor8.

Jennifer Harrison

I am: Interior Stylist, Creative, Flea Market Lover
My home: Euclid, Ohio
My style: One-of-a-Kind. Layered. Free-Spirited with Color and Texture.

My space shows how much I love and appreciate who I am as a stylist/designer.

Jennifer Harrison, also known as Flea Market Fab, has been creatively pursuing her recycled glam style at flea markets, garage sales, and thrift stores for more than a decade. With a playful personality and an eye for the unusual, Jennifer has an unrivaled talent for bringing together spaces that are layered, comfortable, and truly unique.

Jennifer's work has been featured in such print and online publications as *The Jungalow*, *Design Sponge*, *Glitter Guide*, *Do It Yourself Magazine*, *Flea Market Outdoors*, *The Best of Flea Market Style*, and many more.

Your Creative Work

When I was a young girl, my mom would drag me to all the junk spots she would haunt, whether it was a garage sale, antique store, or just a pile of garbage on someone's curb. Since I had this experience and knowledge, it influenced a sort of lifestyle and brand for my life and business. It has been a way of life and continues to influence my design in everything I do, every space, every client . . . it has been my touch, my style.

When I met my husband, he had a company of his own as a concrete contractor. I started helping him run the company and took care of the kids. As they got older and I had more time on my hands, I took my style and passion and started doing what I loved. Since my husband and I built our home and I did all the design work, friends started to refer me. By word of mouth, I started designing spaces and going to clients' homes that needed to be reworked. This became a full-time business, as well as a small company for me.

Your Creative Work Space

I stay true to myself and my style. I allow myself to be open to make fresh changes by buying second hand. You can afford to play when something is one dollar. This allows me to create a space full of one-of-a-kind pieces, cool stuff. My work space fully reflects me and who I am, so I am completely content in my space and office. It's warm and comfortable. Without a doubt, you can walk in and know it's all mine. It's playful and tells a story, which is what I strive for in all my design. I want my things to tell a story.

Staying Organized

This is by far one of the hardest struggles when it comes to working from home. There are so many distractions, and everyday life sometimes interferes. Sticking to a schedule helps. We have certain days we are off and other days we are fully on. Other than that, it's madness. Having a calendar and sticking to it makes for a very productive work environment; you just have to be focused.

Biggest Challenge

Being in the textile business, it can tend to get a bit, oh let me say *dusty*, from all the fibers; so keeping the office clean so that the rest of the house stays clean is by far the biggest struggle. Every day we have to stop an hour early and make sure we clean, organize, and vacuum. Ensuring that gets done makes a huge difference the next day.

Pretty + Practical

Having the ability to score cool pieces of furniture that not only make for a great conversational piece, but also great storage, is the key to success for me. I have a large cabinet that I got for just forty dollars; I found it on craigslist locally from a man who used it in his garage for his tools and supplies. Now I use it for all of our supplies. The drawers are deep, so we store all our shipping supplies, paper, tape, you name it, if it fits, it goes in there.

I also purchased the giant wall units with the cubbies from Ikea. In those boxes, I label and store all of my fabrics and small items. That helps keep it from looking junky.

Core Values

My space shows how much I love and appreciate who I am as a stylist/designer. There isn't a spot in that office that doesn't reflect the time or story it took to find that perfect piece to make the space come to life. I have worked my tail off to be where I am today, and my office reminds me of what it took to get here. It gives me life and happiness to be able to tell my story through a collection.

Sweet Spot Style Tip for Creatives

As long as you stay true to yourself, not what is trendy or being pushed on social media (since that is a persuading channel every day of our lives), you create with what you love. Do *you* and be true to what makes and gives you life and happiness. Your space should be a place that speaks to you and gives you inspiration. Your own inspiration should be your daily driving force.

Best Advice

I have found that having a good support team and goals set months ahead has given me more of a drive to be better. Never doubt yourself; only you can be the success to any story you want to write. Go for it!

Find Jennifer online at fleamarketfab.style
and on Instagram @fleamarketfab.

Joy Cho

I am: Founder and Creative Director of Oh Joy!
My home: Los Angeles, California
My style: Colorful. Feminine.

Living in my sweet spot means that I'm content and happy with where I am in life. I think we are always striving to accomplish more and reach bigger and loftier goals, but I have been working more on not forgetting to appreciate the now and love the things that made today great, too.

Joy Cho is the founder and creative director of the Oh Joy! Brand, which includes a daily lifestyle blog and a licensed product line at Target. She has authored three books and consulted for hundreds of creative businesses around the world. As a graphic designer, Joy originally started her blog, Oh Joy!, as a creative outlet while between jobs. Now she has a global following of over 13 million on all her social media sites combined. Did I mention she's also a mother of two?

Your Creative Work

In 2005, I left my job in New York City to move to Philly for my boyfriend (now my husband). I was in a new city, newly engaged, and looking for a new job. I started my blog as a place to keep my inspirations during a time when I had a lot of transition.

More and more people started to read the site, and it helped me to be able to launch my own design studio due to the clients I was getting from those who read my

blog. I didn't initially plan to start my own business, but once I saw that I could get my own clients, I took the leap of faith. The type of business I was starting (a service-based graphic design business) luckily didn't require much start-up capital. All I needed was a computer, printer, and scanner, all items I already had.

Day in the Life

I start my day by making breakfast for my kids and getting them ready for the day. I bring my older daughter to school and then head in to work. No day is the same, but a typical day usually starts with checking e-mails, staff/client meetings, and getting the more administrative tasks out of the way. In the afternoon, I focus on the creative side of my job by working on editorial content and design projects with help from my team to brainstorm new ideas and make these projects come to life.

I leave the office by 4:00 p.m. to pick up my oldest from school and get home to my little one by 4:30 p.m. Then we hang out, make dinner, and eat together before they are off to bed at 7:00 p.m. During the week, after my kids go to bed, I usually work an additional two to three hours to wrap up things I wasn't able to finish earlier in the day. When you have your own business, it's hard to ever really be done working. But I do try to take off on the weekends and focus on hanging out and being fully present with my family.

Your Creative Work Space

When you're in a space you love and with people you enjoy working with, it makes your day (and your work) that much better.

Our studio is sectioned off in order to function the way we need it to for all the different

things we do at Oh Joy! We have our desk area, we have a few shooting spaces, we have a craft station, and we have areas for us to eat lunch all together as a team. It's one big open space so you can see everything that is going on, but by having sections it helps to keep the creative chaos contained.

Biggest Challenge

The biggest challenge is how to divide up a big open space. While it is beautiful and great for our small team, you also can't hide any messes, and we constantly have work in progress that can't always be put away every day. We also have a lot of props, tons of product samples, and just things in general that we need to create, so storage is always a problem to solve.

Pretty + Practical

We solved the storage problem with lots of big units that we bought inexpensively, but we made them look more lux with knobs or other decorative accents.

Sweet Spot Style Living

It means that I'm content and happy with where I am in life. I think we are always striving to accomplish more and reach bigger and loftier goals, but I have been working more on not forgetting to appreciate the now and love the things that made today great, too.

SMEG Love

I just love it. It's not the biggest fridge, but it's perfect for an office environment.

Style Tips

Think first about functionality and how you (and your team) need to perform on a daily basis. It's often easy to think first about the decorative aspects for a creative space, but function needs to come first, and then decor can be the icing on the cake. Also, keep in mind built-in aspects, like lighting, and how much work you'll need to put in to really make it feel like your own.

Find Oh Joy! on social media @ohjoy or online at ohjoy.com.

Emily Henderson

I am: Stylist, Author, Style Blogger, Target's Home Spokesperson
My home: Los Angeles, California
My style: Happy. Eclectic. Colorful. With a Little Bit of Weird.

Having an office space that feels grown up but still creative allows us to enjoy the space and the creative process.

Oregon bred, New York trained, and based in Los Angeles, Emily Henderson is a home style expert who spends time designing, styling, art directing, running, and writing her blog, all while raising her son and daughter with her husband in Los Angeles.

Emily is currently Target's Home spokesperson and is known for mixing eclectic styles on a moderate budget.

Your Creative Work

After earning a liberal arts degree in Oregon, I moved cross-country to pursue life and success in the Big Apple. But without any clear career direction and bills to pay, I took on a number of odd part-time jobs (bartending and dog walking) before landing a position at Jonathan Adler. From there, I connected with stylists and signed on as an assistant after much persistence. In 2009, I applied to be on HGTV's Design Star, won, and then produced my own show for the network, Secrets of Stylists. Now I work full-time managing my style blog, and I have a staff that helps keep it running. We fill it with original content every single day. I am now the home style expert and spokesperson for Target and have a full client list. We are running a full operation over here, but things continue to evolve and change, which is the thing that I love about what I do. It is fortunately now more about the quality of work than the quantity, as it was when I started.

Your Creative Work Space

For the first time, we have a place that feels organized, inspiring, and really allows us to focus on each project we are doing. The new office has a full library, design areas, a conference table, and each person has their own desk setup, all of which help with productivity and the overall vibe of the office. It finally feels like a grown-up office, and we are all very excited about it.

Staying Organized

When we first moved into the studio three years ago, it felt so big and spacious. It is 1,200 square feet, and with three people that felt ample. Half of the room was taken up by desks, and the other half was used for storage/props and shoots. Since then, we have doubled in bodies and rent the back unit to house anything unsightly because the front space became a total insane ugly mess. It was absolutely not designed. In fact, it was uninspiring and embarrassing. So when *Wood, Naturally* reached out to us about sponsoring a project, we used it as our excuse to finally tackle our studio and install some much-needed shelving. Investing in studio furniture has made us all feel way more proud to be at work, and I honestly think we get more done in this inspiring and organized space.

Biggest Challenge

The biggest challenge we had was dealing with storing samples—tile, fabric, catalogues, etc.— for design clients. We needed to have a decent inventory to save us and our client sourcing time. When you need a lot of closed storage, it's so easy for it to look like a big generic cabinet, so the little details we've added help to give the piece some variation and character. Inside it is temporarily styled out with beautiful things that we need, which will quickly be filled with stuff that we can't throw away as we start to live and work with the piece to fill it up and organize it. It's great to have the closed storage space for the less-than-beautiful things we don't want to look at every day and can cause visual chaos and clutter. And now that we have a larger design staff, we actually have someone dedicated to keeping things categorized and organized in the office and these cabinets.

Pretty + Practical

We installed simple art ledges so that we could display some of the mood boards from current projects we are working on. We had the copper ladder custom made by our welder for $250, and it's perfect to break up the space between the dressers, create a soft/sculptural piece for your eye, and to hang pretty fabrics and samples on. We installed our old sconces from the other side of the office above the dressers to round off the space and add more lighting in the winter when people are in the office past sundown. We also used some super simple pulls that we painted rose gold after playing around with a few other colors. White looked annoying, black looked contemporary. We could have done something leather, but we didn't have time and weren't sure how those would hold up with the amount of use they would get. These are super streamlined and pretty.

Sweet Spot Style Living

Life is all about finding the right balance. It is still a juggling act for me, with two young ones and a full-time job and design studio, but I have learned to delegate what I can't do—or don't have time to do—to my wonderful staff, which allows me to spend more time with my family and focus on those projects that do need my attention.

Core Values

We *love* this studio now. It's such a happier/better place to be and one that we are proud of, not embarrassed about. It is a bit playful, but not crazy. And the best part—it's *wildly* more functional. All our desks are on the other side of the room, and this side serves as the design library and meeting/conference area. My mantra is and has always been: Perfection is boring, let's get weird. Having an office space that feels grown up but still creative allows us to enjoy the space and the creative process.

Style Tips

Invest in those pieces that will help you to stay organized. There is nothing worse in an office than trying to remember where you threw the tape measure, or the paint chips, or the extra Post-it notes. Once you are organized, you will be surprised by how much time you used to waste trying to find what you needed. If possible, customized shelving and furniture pieces for storage and function will really help the business out! But, big box stores also have some great options that allow you to get and stay organized. Just remember to keep it simple, pretty, and full of function.

Find Emily online at stylebyemilyhenderson.com
and on Instagram @em_henderson.

Jorge Almada and Anne-Marie Midy

We are: Designers, Owners of Casamidy
Our home: Sonora and San Miguel de Allende, México; Brussels, Belgium; Paris, France
Our style: Artisan-Made. Contemporary. Diverse.

Don't buy disposable furniture!

Anne-Marie Midy and Jorge Almada—French and Mexican, respectively—design modern furniture and accessories that are made using traditional techniques by craftsmen in Mexico for sale through their design company, *Casamidy*. I was lucky enough to visit their amazing home in San Miguel de Allende, Mexico, and absolutely fell in love with what I saw. While I haven't been to Sonora, Mexico, I was intrigued by the deep family history that seems to pull this family to the desert.

Your Creative Work

We started *Casamidy* in 1998. We realized soon after college that if we wanted the freedom to design, we would have to find and develop our own manufacturing source. Moving to Mexico was a logical choice, as we were aware of the rich and diverse artisanal traditions. All our production is based in San Miguel de Allende, Mexico.

What is it like working at the ranch with no electricity or Internet?
Things move at a slower pace. For example, once a year I do a general mailing. I like addressing the cards by hand. It takes about eight days. I sit at the dining table with my music ... it goes surprisingly fast. I then load the cards into our old Land Rover and cross the border in order to mail them from the U.S. post office in Bisbee, Arizona. It makes an otherwise tedious process an adventure of sorts.

Tell us about the decision to build your house in the remote Sonora Desert. What pulled you there?
We had a ranch in that area when I was a kid. After having my own kids, I felt an urgent need to return there. Thanks to my aunt, Alejandra Redo, I was able to build something on her property after my dad's death in 2012.

How does being in different locations influence or inspire your creativity?
Yes. At the time we moved to Belgium, I felt Mexico as an inspiration was exhausted for us. Belgium is an enigmatic, sometimes contradictory place, which has rich artistic traditions. It is essential for us to use travel as a source of inspiration for our work. Basically, we work in three ways:

1.   We design things for our home that we feel don't exist.

Jorge and Anne-Marie have added creative little work spaces in their home, like this one in the bedroom.

2. We design things based on travel.

3. We design things inspired by materials and certain artisan techniques.

Staying Organized

Jorge: The trick for me is to delete and trash things every day. I only like displaying twenty-five messages on my email account, for example. Anne-Marie has all her paperwork in plastic sleeves in binders. I keep sketchbooks religiously, as I believe it is important to revisit old ideas. It's particularly important to finish the sketchbooks so you can understand your own thought process.

Biggest Challenge

Anne-Marie and I do not directly collaborate on designs. The most important thing for us is that we each have our own private place to work. As a detail, I like to work over saddle leather. I use one of our Altamura leather-topped desks.

Pretty + Practical

I keep everything in leather pouches. As I travel a lot, I need to be able to fit my desktop into a bag and a backpack. Having different pouches helps me easily identify things.

Core Values

For us, a workplace must be peaceful beyond everything else. Because our lives are busy with our kids, the times we can really sit down and work have become very reduced, so our workplace has to be a sanctuary of sorts.

Tips for Creatives

Take a basic business class so you can avoid making basic mistakes. It's not really something you can do on the side or while you have a full-time job. It's scary, but you just have to take the plunge.

You can find Casamidy online at casamidy.com.

Justina Blakeney

I am: Designer, Artist, Mama, Founder of The Jungalow
My home: Los Angeles, California
My style: Jungalicious. Patternful. Bohemian.

If I look at something and it's something I love, it doesn't matter if it's old or new. It's just about a certain magnetism that a lot of items have—a sense of soul and a sense of beauty.

Justina Blakeney, founder of *The Jungalow*, has taken personal branding to a whole new level with an outreach of 1.9 million to date. She's been named as Instagram's Top Designer to Follow by *Harper's Bazaar* and *Lonny* magazine and has worked with brands such as Anthropologie, 1stdibs, One Kings Lane, eBay, CB2, Microsoft, West Elm, Airbnb, and Joss & Main. She's also the author of the New York Times best-selling book *The New Bohemians*.

I've been following Justina for some time. In fact, she was featured in my first book, and I had the opportunity to meet her in person at her creative workshop in Cinque Terre, Italy.

In case you're wondering, she is just as cool off-line as she is online. What I really admire about Justina is how she's created a unique boho aesthetic that truly reflects her core essence.

For Justina, decorating is about feeling free, having fun, and getting a little bit wild. She currently lives in Los Angeles in her plant-filled bungalow, or "Jungalow," as she calls it, with her husband and young daughter, Ida.

Your Creative Work Space

I was working from home, and as my business expanded I felt I really needed my own separate studio/office space where I could focus on my creative work. So, I found this amazing 700-square-foot warehouse space that's only a block from my home. This space, with its high ceilings and great light, was perfect. Beyond its physical attributes, being in this particular space is a sign that I'm dedicated to my vision. I'm always striving to reach my *North Star*, or my ultimate vision. Being here inspires me to keep heading in the right direction.

Staying Organized

I have lots of tchotchkes and need lots of stuff for styling shoots. I love collecting textiles, vintage items, and botanicals. By my desk, I have a utility desk with open drawers to keep everyday items handy, such as my Pigma

Micron pens, watercolors and watercolor paper, scissors, graph paper, sticky notes, and such. I have open shelving to display my beloved textiles, and I keep paperwork filed away, because who wants to see that?

One of my favorite tricks is my signature shelf display. Right now it's a coral shelf with a circle painted on the wall. I place one or two items there that I want to highlight. When your space is full of cool stuff, try this style trick. It allows your eye to rest and focus on one special piece. The beauty of this shelf is that you can change the focus item as often as you'd like.

Core Values

Growth over perfection is my motto. You'll get better the more you create, not the more you think about it. I also strongly believe that your pocketbook should not dictate your style. In other words, you don't have to be wealthy to have style, but you do need creativity.

Sweet Spot Style Living

I seek to feel fully engaged, grateful, energetic, like a boss, lucky, passionate, excited, gangster, creative.

Did you ever have doubts about being a lady boss?

I've always felt drawn to having my own business. Early on, I created my own fashions and had a boutique in Italy. The financial piece can be scary, but I've always been a *follow-your-heart* kind of gal. I can't imagine it any other way.

Tips for Creatives

Find your own North Star and take small daily actions toward your big goals. Don't worry if you don't see immediate results. It's taken years for my career to evolve into what it is today. Keep in good company with like-minded folks who can support you. Let your creative passions guide you.

Nonnegotiable Style Element

If I had to choose one thing, I'd say botanicals. Plants bring life to any space. They stimulate the senses and bring that wild essence, which is so iconic for me. It's what makes the Jungalow the Jungalow.

As a working mom myself, I'm curious how you organize your time to get so much done while still devoting time to your family.

I struggle with that, too. I'm pretty lucky in the sense that my husband is a stay-at-home dad and both sets of grandparents live in LA, so we have lots of support and I have an awesome creative team. That's essential. I also have some ground rules. I don't work on the weekends, and we always do bath and bedtime together every night, so that's really special. Even though I love to work, I want to maintain a certain lifestyle, and that means spending quality time with those I love. It also means taking care of myself. I hit the spa a couple of times a month if I can and bring my little one with me. We love mommy–daughter dates.

Best Advice

The best advice I ever received was from my mother. She said to pick your partners by people that you can grow together with. I think about that every time I'm hiring someone new for the business, and I thought a lot about that before Jason and I got married. A healthy relationship is one that supports growth in business and in life.

Find Justina online at thejungalow.com
and on Instagram @justinablakeney and @thejungalow.

Amy Rouse

I am: Owner of Green Body + Green Home
My home: Tampa, Florida
My style: Minimal. Bohemian.

Living in my sweet spot, to me, means knowing in your gut that you're doing what you were meant to do.

Amy Rouse is the founder of Green Body + Green Home, a brand formed out of the desire to offer green, ethical products. Locally, Green Body + Green Home offers skin care treatments and massage. The retail and online shop carries an array of home decor and beautiful personal accessories, all carefully curated based on Amy's desire to offer unique green products to the home and beyond.

Your Creative Work

Looking back, I can see that I have always been interested in design, it just took me a while to realize it. I remember as a child asking my father to cut down some low-lying limbs from a tree in our front yard so I could create a "house" with different rooms that I could decorate. In college I took a few interior design courses but ended up graduating with a degree in philosophy.

From there I simply explored the world. I took a five-month road trip around the country, took some photography classes, and curated local art shows. I landed on massage therapy as a career because I knew I was good at it. I built a strong practice over the next eighteen years but never lost the desire to create beautiful spaces. The way my studio space felt to my clients was almost as important as the massage itself. The lighting, music, and decor all impacted how my clients received the treatment and ultimately made me stand out from the other therapists in town.

I took a break from massage when my girls were born to focus on them, but I became very restless. After a summer in Spain, I returned to the States and took a job at the local Anthropologie store as a visual sales assistant. This was the pivot point for me. What I learned there about merchandising and installation ignited my creativity, and I knew that the design world was where I wanted to be.

I went back into the massage business knowing that the client base I had established would be the source to feed my new business endeavor, combining massage, skin care, and interior design, all three focused on green, ethical products. I am at heart a minimalist, so if you're going to buy something, it should provide a fair living for the people whose talent and skill go into those products, provide the consumer with a quality product that is hard to find in mass-produced products, and be environmentally friendly.

Your Creative Work Space

My creative work space is my studio. Combining massage and skin care services with a retail studio and interior styling services isn't as easy as it sounds. It is a dream job for sure, but it is demanding. I recently expanded my studio so that I could do more things with less effort. The majority of my retail sales are online, and since most of my products are one-of-a-kind pieces, I was constantly having to update my website.

I was using my home as my photography studio, lugging all the rugs and pillows to my house, tearing my house apart for photo shoots, then having to bring it all back to the studio. I wanted to create a space that would eliminate all that work. So we expanded the studio and set it up so that one side of the studio was allowed to change—that was my photography set. I have great lighting and tall ceilings, so it was more than an ideal situation.

Now I have a space that is ever-changing, and clients look forward to seeing what I've done. A common comment is "Every time I come in it's different," which I love!

Staying Organized

Ha! I'm still learning that trick. One thing I hate more than anything is wasted time. I'm always looking for a better way to do everything. Because the business is constantly growing and changing, it's hard to stick with one system of organization. I find that everything must be written down or it does not get done. If someone asks me for anything, I ask that they put it in writing, otherwise I cannot be held responsible. A text or email works best.

When you own your own business, there is a constant swirl in your head of things that need to be done. It can be extremely overwhelming and stressful, so when it gets too crazy, I allow myself to *not* do something. I tell myself the world is not going to end if I don't respond to that email. I also work better if my work space and home are clean and uncluttered. So on a regular basis I purge. I purge paperwork, clothes, furniture, just about anything that's not nailed down. The less stuff I have to deal with, the more time I have, period!

Biggest Challenge

The biggest challenge I have at the studio is storage. I have dedicated a lot of space for the treatment rooms and built a break room for my staff, which left me with little storage.

I am currently investing in some storage pieces that will help the organization and flow of the space. There are some great storage solutions at Ikea that you can customize, including shelves and drawers, too! Right now the break room is a dumping ground, and I want it to be a retreat for my staff to relax in. I need to hide the clutter!

Pretty + Practical

Furniture that doubles as storage—best thing ever! There should be function in pretty things, especially if you are working with limited space. My most favorite possession ever is a 200-year-old rice table from Bali that has a ridiculous amount of storage. It lives in the studio and is a true conversation piece that offers me a place to store office supplies and extra inventory while being beautiful (see photo).

Amy utilizes nontraditional means of storage, such as this 200-year-old rice table from Bali.

Sweet Spot Style Living

Sweet spot to me means knowing in your gut that you're doing what you were meant to do. I had that feeling on my first design job. I was nervous as hell that I was going to look like an idiot and be called out for my lack of experience. The first meeting with the contractor was pure magic. All my fears fell away and I just dove in like I knew what I was doing, and I guess I did because the project turned out amazing. I remember going home that evening and telling my husband I nailed it and that this is what I was meant to do. That's the sweet spot, when you nail it and it feels so good!!

Core Values

My entire business is based on my core values. Do no harm. Love yourself and others. Mindful consumerism may be a new catchphrase now, but I have always tried to live by this motto. It hasn't been easy, and I have failed at times because the price is just too good to pass up.

But I have learned that it's better to wait and have nothing than to have a bunch of cheaply made things that are a waste of our precious resources.

The products we use in our services are all eco-friendly and contain no harmful chemicals. All of the retail products we sell are ethically sourced and provide a fair living to the artisans who make them. When I see similar products in the bigger retail stores for a fraction of the cost, I realize how hard it can be to not buy them—I am even tempted to buy them myself. Having this business has forced me to walk the walk, and for that I am grateful.

Style Tips

Be patient. It doesn't happen overnight. Be mindful of your purchases, make sure you are buying quality pieces that will last and serve a purpose. Don't just buy it because it's pretty. You will end up getting frustrated with this pretty thing because it is not serving your purpose. It's okay to have empty space, just make sure it is balanced. By balance, I'm talking about empty space so that your eye and mind can rest. For example, if you have a tall plant or piece of furniture filling one side of the wall, you can leave the space next to it empty, but balance or ground it with a lower piece of furniture.

Find Amy online at palma-living.com
and on Instagram @palma.living.

IT'S ALL I
TO BRING

THIS, AND

RT BE

THIS, AND MY
AND ALL THE

AND ALL
MEADOWS

Jo Chattman

I am: Photographer, Stylist
My home: Greenfield, Massachusetts
My style: Ethereal. Vintage. Collected.

My entire studio is designed to help me be in my best mental state to work on my images and create. I surround myself with comfort and support, and I think that really puts me in a good head space creativitywise.

I was so excited to discover Jo Chattman, who lives very close to me in the neighboring town of Greenfield, Massachusetts. Jo is an incredibly talented and sought-after photographer and stylist, and her studio is simply stunning.

Your Creative Work

I studied photography at Parsons and then fell into being a studio manager for a commercial still life photographer. For the next five years, I stuck with it because I simply didn't know what else to do. Yet, through this experience I learned so many things that help me in my work today. I gained experience in just about every part of the advertising industry, as well as the business side of things. I learned how to estimate jobs, negotiate fees, maintain client relationships, hire freelancers, and really get a good grasp on all the aspects of a large production.

From there, I decided to try my hand at styling for advertising because I was always good at making things look good. The photographer I was working for noticed

that and encouraged me. I've always been good at interpreting what kind of
look a director is going for and how styling and choice of light, location, props,
and models work together.

I did really well in the field, but I always wanted to be behind the camera.

I found myself styling for all male photographers, which was a little weird. I
was like, *where are all the female photographers?*

When I was about thirty, I decided I really needed to be behind the lens and
start taking the shots. I felt confident in my ability, and the world was much
more open to female photographers than it was in the nineties. I also live in a
super liberal wonderful community and had lots of help and encouragement
from them getting started. (Love you Happy Valley!)

Now I mentor young female photographers and usually hire all-girl teams
to help even the playing field. Even today, people still tend to only hire male
assistants because of a variety of dumb reasons. So my own little piece of
active feminism in response to that is hiring kick-ass, smart ladies.

I have found that they are versatile and help me with aesthetic decisions and styling if I need them to as well, which is cool. Don't get me wrong, I do hire men sometimes, but I remember how hard it was for me to learn because of sexist attitudes, so I try to help my sisters out when possible. I like teaching them how to value themselves and their work as photographers so they can make a living.

I'm currently working with a variety of clients, and that's what I love. One day I'm working in Malibu for a corporate fashion client, the next for a smaller textile designer that's local. I love the variety!

Making meaningful connections and building trusting professional friendships is really important to me and has helped guide me in the types of clients I choose to work with. Aside from my commercial work, I pick ten weddings to photograph a year because I adore being part of a beautiful celebration and then surprising couples with their day as I see it unfold.

It's very satisfying and makes me happy. I love my couples so much … they bring great joy and friendship into my life, even after the wedding. Lately I've been shooting weddings for a few people at the Free People [clothing brand] headquarters. I love working with them because they all are so creative. I also have a lot of wedding couples who are photographers, and I actually love the pressure to impress and delight them.

Staying Organized

It's a challenge because I am a collector. If you take pictures for a living, Adobe Lightroom is the single best organizational tool. If nothing else, my images are organized.

The rest of my life is more fluid, and generally things kind of look happily disorganized. I'm the opposite of Marie Kondo [organizing consultant and author of *The Life-Changing Magic of Tidying Up*]. I like looking around and seeing layers of stuff I love.

I also connect emotion with certain objects, so those become sentimental. I believe objects have lives and histories. However, I am not the type of person to get the least bit upset if my dog or son (it's usually one of them) ruins something expensive. I justify it by thinking, *its time was up*, and I can usually replace the item if I really want to.

Core Values

I work with great people. I think that's the single biggest reflection of my values. In New York, I felt trapped working with many people I didn't like on a personal level. There were a few good eggs, but in general I was dismayed and discouraged to see how people in the advertising industry behaved. Now that I have more control, I make sure I like the people I work with. Working there has made me a better boss today, though, so I guess that's a silver lining.

I also learned how not to behave with my team. I pay my workers super quickly and advocate for our projects to be paid. I never expect anything for free from anyone. I also treat them with respect and promote them in their own careers. Kindness goes a long way!

I admire my clients. I will try extra hard and put in 110 percent of myself and creativity for a client I love, so my work and style continues to grow as well from this. Generally, I can assess whether a client is a good match for me after a few emails. I trust my instincts.

Sweet Spot Living

It can be anywhere as long as my husband, son, and dogs are close by, but it needs to be my own space. My creative work space is a sanctuary from my home life and all that is happening in the world. When curating my things, I look for things that will not make me cringe when I look at them and think *I have to get on that*. It's distracting to have a lot of stuff like that in your creative space. I try to simplify what I surround myself with.

My space is tailored to how
I like to work and see things.
For example, I like burning a
little Palo Santo when I come
into work. If I need a break
from focus, I can play with
my dogs because they are a
loving support and my studio
companions. I also adore my
plants. Each one is special and
given to me by good friends.
Some are more than seventy-
five years old!

Vintage factory worktables
from local mills that have been
shut down make great surfaces
to spread out on, look at work,
and take inventory of products
in the light. Card catalogs are
great for storing the million odds and ends I collect. Most important, good
light from the windows is essential. To help with mood and ambiance, I added
a chandelier.

Baskets, pots, textiles, and an amazing watering can all came from my friend
Eliza's store, Kestrel, in Northampton (see resource guide). I'm lucky, because
I have lots of odds and ends hanging around from shoots I do with Ode
Boutique and photo shoots with my adventure girlfriend, Kristin.

That Secret Holiday Banner is something she commissioned for Ode
Boutique's spring window display, and now it lives in my studio. She's an
amazing writer and poet and always thinking up the coolest projects. The
quote on the banner is one she chose from Emily Dickinson.

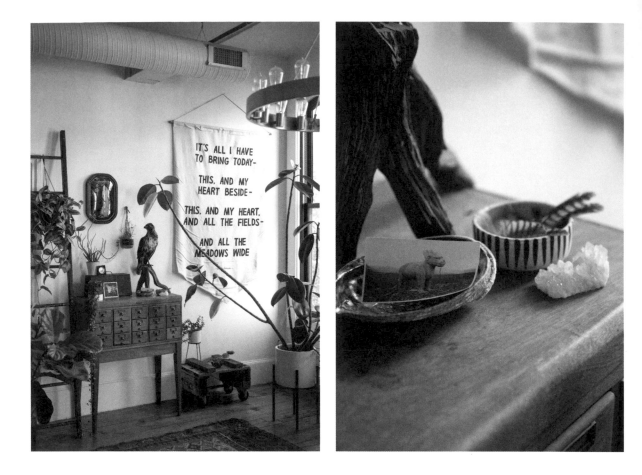

In my studio, you'll always hear music. It brings such energy to the space. You can follow me on Spotify (Joanna Chattman) if you wish to hear what I'm currently editing and shooting to. I love making playlists and sharing music with friends.

I also love to have pieces of my clients' work. I work with lots of jewelers, textile designers, and ceramic artists and like to display their work around the studio. Most of my working relationships are actually friendships that mean a lot to me, so having a little piece of their work reminds me of that person.

Nonnegotiable Style Element

Surround yourself with what you love. I rarely look at Pinterest or media for decorating my own space. I tailor it to who I am and what brings me happiness.

Style Tip

Make it a functional sanctuary for yourself. Invest in your space and in yourself. Sometimes a corner of the dining room doesn't cut it. For me, I was lucky to have a wise friend who told me I needed to invest in myself and get a good space. It was a risk, but it has made all the difference in how I feel when I go to work.

Look for Jo on her website, chattmanphotography.com, and on Instagram @ jochat.

Create Your Sweet Spot Study or Dream Nook

It's not that common anymore for folks to say, *I'm going to retire to the library*. Hearing that, you might conjure a dark paneled room with Victorian chairs, loads of dark shelves lined with leather-bound books, and perhaps a mahogany desk adorned with a cigar box and a flask of whiskey tucked in a desk drawer.

I think we should bring the library back, but with a feminine touch.

There's a room downstairs—I can't call it my office since that's upstairs in my bedroom now—but the room that was formerly my office is now much more of a library or study. Really, it's a dream nook. It's where I go to have a cup of tea, look over my favorite home decor books, write in my vision books, and dream.

Albert Einstein said that imagination is more important than knowledge, and I believe that to be true. We are all so *busy* these days that no one is taking enough time to simply dream. I personally require quite a bit of white space in my life. As a mother and entrepreneur, I have a full plate, but I know that taking time out to relax, reflect, dream, and plan is essential for me to become the woman I aspire to be.

It's simple to create a dream nook. You really just need a cozy chair, a place to rest your tea or coffee cup, and permission to allow yourself to go there.

Permission granted.

At left, you can get a feel for my dream nook filled with the things I love: decor books, vision journals, art, plants, and sunlight.

*This hutch from Ikea serves as a pretty place
to hold my office supplies and books.*

Don't forget to add some green to your sweet spot space. Botanicals produce oxygen, which is good to clear the air and your mind.

Art and handmade objects personalize a space. The nudes were a gift from my friend Catalina Rodriquez. See page 81 for her story. The stone bird is by another artist friend, Erin Larkin. The basket is from a market in Tunisia. I picked up the handmade Mexican wrestler doll in a little shop in Playa del Carmen, Mexico, El Jaguar Dorado.

the artist's studio

For All Sorts of Creators

Who gets excited about art? I do! I love visiting art studios. It just feels good. Stepping into someone's creative studio is a special treat that shows a glimpse of what life is like for an artist. I think everyone is creative, but some are more dedicated to their art than others, and you can often tell by taking a look at *where* they create. In this section, we have a beautiful blend of creative spaces for the multitalented artist. There are painters, graphic designers, illustrators, a textile designer, and a color energy expert.

At left, Amira Rahim at work on a canvas.

Catalina Rodriguez

I am: Artist, Designer, Pharmacist, Environmental Engineer
My home: Santiago de Compostela, Spain
My style: Vibrant. Natural. Spontaneous.

Don't let fear prevent you from doing what you like.

I met Catalina at a workshop in Italy and we hit it off!
Catalina is a shining star with a generous and lovely spirit.

Your Creative Work

I have to admit that it is difficult to find a balance. Since I work full time as an air quality technician, I carve out time for my art mainly in the afternoons, evenings, and weekends. The thing is that painting lights me up. I'm not happy when I am not doing it. But when you dedicate time to your passion, it's really not such a sacrifice. All I want to do is create all day! I have learned to get my daily duties done quickly so I can devote most of my time to do what I love. Having said this, when I have an exhibition, balance goes out the window, and it's all about the art!

Biggest Challenge

Time. I became ambitious about having as much creative time as I could gather. Most of the time I feel I am running all day. I really miss time to slow down, think, read, research, and do things without rushing. Yet, even if there were forty-eight hours in the day, I'd still fill them fully, and I bet I'd feel the same way. Even though it's a challenge, I choose not to complain. I'm doing this because I love it.

Your Creative Work Space

My studio is in my home. The walls and the main furniture are white because white makes me feel calm and peaceful so that I can add color with my decor and my art. I have a big white desk in the living room and work there or on the floor. There is plenty of light entering from a window gallery full of plants in my living room. I love decorating with plants because it reminds me of my mom. She always had a beautiful garden full of flowers. Botanicals give a home life.

I use the wall behind my table as an inspirational mood board that I change constantly.

Because my living room space is full of ideas, inspiration, and stimulation, I keep my bedroom clear and minimal with just some books, a couple of candles, and a lamp. I feel my space mimics my mind, so it's important for me that my bedroom is a clean and quiet place, free of clutter so that my mind can relax.

Artwork is challenging. The better I feel about the place where I create, the better results I get. I love creating in my home studio and surrounding myself with as much beauty as I can.

Practical + Pretty

You know what happens when you have chocolates around, don't you? You eat them! I really need to have my things out and handy, so that it's easy to get started. Luckily, I have plenty of wardrobes [closets], so when I have guests or need to tidy up to start a new project, I can store them for a while very quickly. After that, I need everything out again.

I love to have my pencils and brushes in glass or ceramic vases. I also have a small collection of bowls for working with watercolors and inks.

Staying Focused

When I started painting professionally, I tried to make one thing at a time, but it didn't work for me. Multitasking is a reflection of my personality. I'm a multi-passionate, curious, impatient, and somewhat obsessive person. I prefer to have at least two things on-site to keep me proactive and focused. I'm the same way with books. I always read at least two books at a time. I feel much more inspired this way, and the results I get are better.

Sweet Spot Style Living

As I see it, it's a lifestyle choice. It's not about having the bigger or better house or studio. It's about creating and owning your space. You are going to spend a lot of time there, so you might as well enjoy it.

The space could be only one desk or a corner, as long as it represents you. That's why I use my walls as a big inspiration board. That's why I'm surrounded by plants and books at home. I'm planning to do a big mural on one of my walls. I love my home and studio, but the truth is I've created a sweet spot in every place I've lived because I consciously create it that way. I'm always adding details to my space that cheer me up and inspire me. That's what sweet spot style is to me.

Best Advice

Don't let fear prevent you from doing what you like. It is a cliché, but so true. Don't let anybody discourage you. Follow your intuition. I mean, give it a real chance. Avoid negative people and think positive! As Elizabeth Gilbert says in her book *Big Magic: Creative Living Beyond Fear*, "The guardians of high culture will try to convince you that the arts belong only to a chosen few, but they are wrong and they are also annoying."

Dream big, work hard.

Find Catalina at catalamitad.com, on Instagram @catalamitad, or via email at catalamitad@gmail.com.

Louise Gale

I am: Color Energy Artist, Creative Guide
My home: Costa Del Sol, Spain
My style: Calm. Neutral. Big Pops of Expressive Color.

Living in my sweet spot means having the freedom to choose how I spend my day.

Louise Gale is an artist, color energy expert, author, and all-around positive-spirited sweetheart. Louise is from Britain but lives in sunny Spain now. She's been featured all over the Internet and is a regular contributor to *MOYO* magazine. Her new book, *Mandala for the Inspired Artist*, came out in 2016.

Your Creative Work

Color is so essential to our lives. Each and every color of the rainbow—red, orange, yellow, green, blue, indigo, and violet—has its own energy vibration and essentially healing power, which we can all absorb in various ways, such as the clothes we wear, the food we eat, and how we decorate our home.

Colors will affect us differently emotionally, physically, and mentally, and although each color has its own energy vibration and color psychology, every one of us also has our own individual relationship with color. This can be related to how our eye perceives the color vibration, colors triggering childhood memories, or the culture in which we grew up.

When I create, I approach my work with a specific intention of using particular energies of color to infuse the work with that energy, primarily based on color psychology, but also from an intuitive place of knowing how color is linked to our own energy system we call the chakras. When I paint, I am very aware of the impact the colors are having on me and others.

As a color energy artist, I want to create colorful art that stirs something positive inside of people: a feeling, emotion, memory, or a knowing that color will balance them or heal something inside of them. For example, a blue painting is perfect to bring a calm, relaxing feeling to a room. Red sparks passion into the bedroom, and yellow can stimulate the mind in an office.

In addition to painting, I love to share my passion and knowledge of color energy through articles, books, and resources. I also host a variety of creative online classes and write about my painting process to inspire and guide others to explore their own creativity and story with color.

You have a gorgeous studio with an ocean view. What brought you to Spain?

In my early twenties, I remember standing on top of a big hill in awe, overlooking the sea on the coast of Spain, saying to myself, *I am going to live in Spain one day.* Although at the time I had no idea how that could even be possible, the universe was most certainly listening. Twenty years later, a friend invited me to visit Costa Del Sol for the month of August. I was desperate to escape the New York City summer heat, and so it started.

The universe conspired and set the wheels in motion. I was not even contemplating a move in 2010, but when I returned in August 2011, many serendipitous meetings, conversations, and universal magic happened, and I started to crave a simpler life. When I came back in August 2012, I was ready for a change, and it was then that the universe presented my opportunity. There were a few obstacles, but I had faith that it would all work out. And it did! Three weeks later, I signed the papers for my lovely little space of joy, which, by the way, is right next door to my friend!

The stunning view from Louise's studio (Costa Del Sol, Spain).

Color

Every morning, the first thing I do is pull up my blind, look at my wonderful view, and say good morning to it. It is so inspiring with the blues of the sky and the sea, the clean white Spanish cottages below, and pops of colorful bougainvillea and hibiscus peeking out. The colors outside tend to stay the same all year round, apart from a beautiful steely gray that appears when it is stormy in the winter.

The studio is east facing, so the sun always greets me. In the summer, this brings a hot sizzle into the studio. In the winter, it is a welcoming heat that warms those winter mornings with golden light.

During the summer, my studio is full of calming cool blue paintings on the walls and thin curtains that let the light shine through. This brings tranquility to my work and cools the temperature in the summer. During the winter, I opt for deeper, warmer colors that include fuchsia pink and violet, so small changes in the season really do impact the colors I create in and have around me.

In summary, *all* of this influences my creative work, from the colors I choose to paint to how I want to feel in my studio space, which is light, airy, warm, and inspired!

Staying Organized

I love my little studio space, but when I am painting, my studio does not always look very organized at all. The floor is covered with a drop sheet, and it becomes a scene of organized chaos!

When I am working on a particular project such as an e-course or book, one way I love to stay organized and on task is to pin big pieces of paper to the wall. I map out my months ahead, plotting the main milestones and monthly goals. I also have a colorful desk planner, which is my day-to-day schedule that I use and carry everywhere I go to jot down ideas and help me juggle.

I tend to work on lots of projects at once, so my studio sometimes morphs to support what I am working on at the time. And although it's a small space, it has dedicated areas for painting, writing, and contemplating.

For storage, I have a big art supply cupboard in the corner of the studio that is ready to burst, so when I open that, it is piled high with a less-than-beautiful balancing act in there!

Sweet Spot Style Living

Living in my sweet spot means having the freedom to choose how I spend my day. I love to live a simple life but also have it filled with fun, creative projects, inspiring people, and time to rejuvenate in nature. Living in my sweet spot also means having space—beautiful physical space and meditative calming headspace.

Core Values

I approach everything I do with positive energy. This shows up by being true to the work I choose to do in the world, making time to create, and working with people who have good energy, too.

I keep my studio (and life!) as clear and free of clutter as much as I can, which usually means I am constantly clearing, which I love to do. I use a smudge stick (which is traditionally dried white sage tied together), light the end of it so it smokes, and then in a circular motion move it around the rooms in each corner and along the walls. This adds negative ions to the room, which actually creates a more positive atmosphere. It also clears negative energy. I am learning about feng shui at the moment and love how all of these aspects of color and energy come together. When I clear my space with sage like this, I most certainly see a difference in my artwork.

Color Tips

A creative space is one that inspires but is also arranged so that it optimizes the work you do there. Color can affect us all differently, so the first thing to do is to really get to know how color feels to you. Collect different color swatches, paint chips, or cutouts from magazines and keep them in your creative space to *try them on*. Ask yourself how this color/shade/hue makes you feel.

This is so important, especially before you decide to paint a large space in any particular color.

Some creatives work well in a plain, sparsely decorated space, helping to clear the mind and also providing a blank canvas to add to. Others crave a more busy, colorful space that constantly gives them energy. Create an inspiration wall with images and colors that inspire you and motivate you to get started. Only paint large spaces in a color that you absolutely adore and that provides the right energy for you and your creative projects.

Explore colors that invoke the feelings you want to have while you create. For example, a relaxing watery blue shade for calmness, a pink for more compassion, or perhaps a violet to help you get in touch with your spiritual side. You can also be creative with color in how you introduce it into your space. A hot pink chair or a bright yellow plant pot can bring fun color to your creative day.

Tips For Creatives

I have always found that when I follow the path of my heart, the universe conspires to help create the life or outcome I envision. There are ebbs and flows, of course, so staying positive and living more in the present moment has always helped me through transitional periods or times of uncertainty.

Here are the three main tips I'd like to share that enabled me to create a sweet spot life that I still use today:

1. Identify that particular something you love and give yourself permission to carve out time for it every day; it may only be ten minutes to begin with. As long as it gives you joy, it will change your day. Prioritize your day; it will set the scene for the future. As we say in Spain, *poco a poco*, or little by little.

2. Be clear about the direction you want to travel in and the life you want to have. Create a vision board, brainstorm with friends, declutter every area of your life, and find your place of balance. Ask yourself questions, challenge your thinking, and find clarity. You get to make the choices to create your dream life.

3. Be thankful for what you already have and see the beauty in every moment. Gratitude vibrates the highest level of energy, and if you believe in the law of attraction of like attracting like, more good vibes will always come your way. This. Changes. Everything.

"Creativity is the natural order of life. Life is energy: pure creative energy."
—Julia Cameron

Find Louise online at louisegale.com, on Instagram @louisegale, or on Facebook at LouiseGaleArtandDesign.

Flora Bowley

I am: Painter, Workshop Facilitator, Author, Inspirationalist
My home: Portland, Oregon
My style: Brave. Intuitive. Heartfelt.

I believe passionately in every human's ability to create, and I know deep down in my bones that creative expression is a crucial part of holistic well-being. That's why I've always done whatever I needed to do to keep creating. During one particularly romantic summer, I even camped in a national forest and painted in my nearby storage unit.

Artistic pursuits, such as painting, have the power to soothe, heal, and connect a person to their truest self. For author Flora Bowley, making art and expressing herself creatively have always served as potent forms of personal evolution and holistic healing. Flora paints and teaches painting in her Portland studio and around the globe.

Your Creative Work

It's so interesting looking back, because I never used to see how all my passions [yoga, healing, nature, art] overlapped until I started teaching. Instinctively, I combined movement, meditation, nature, and painting into my first workshop because it all just made sense that way. Now I realize that all these parts of myself really *do* live in the same room in my heart, and the way that I combine them creates a really unique experience for my students.

I think when we find these overlaps in our interests, they are able to feed one another more and more. I also think these unique combinations allow us to step more solidly on our life's path.

Your Creative Work Space

As an artist, Libra, and sensitive soul, my physical work space has a tremendous effect on me. When I was looking for a new studio to host my workshops in Portland, I knew I found it the second I walked in the door. Eighteen hundred square feet with tall ceilings, exposed brick, wood floors, and industrial warehouse windows set the stage for a truly dreamy workshop space. When my students aren't there, I just get to dance around a lot!

In addition to the lovely space itself, there are a few important things I added to really make it feel like my own. The first thing I did was to install an awesome surround sound stereo system. Music is a crucial part of my workshops, and having really good sound makes all the difference. My ever-evolving hanging altar also serves as an important element in the space by reminding everyone to stay connected to spirit as we move through the ups and downs of the brave, intuitive painting process.

Other key aspects of the space include globe lights, string lights, plants, fresh flowers, candles, books, a tea bar, yoga props, comfy paint-covered furniture, and individual paint carts for each student. All of these little touches make for a really sweet, nurturing, and inspiring work space. I often hear my students say they want to move in!

How does being in your current studio help you create the work you were meant to do?

I've certainly created in every kind of space imaginable. I've painted in a storage unit, basements, garages, corners of bedrooms, and backyard shacks. While some of these spaces were decidedly not glamorous, I always delighted in making each space feel really special by adding all my sweet little touches and good intentions—no big budget required.

I will say one thing I really love about my current space is how *big* it is. While I definitely don't need all that space for myself, it does give me a sense of expanded possibility—like anything is possible because there's simply enough room to hold it all. I also love vibing off all the great energy that my students create in the workshops. I feel like they are there with me even when I'm alone.

Day in the Life

At this point in my business, my studio is a crucial element, because I'm teaching about seven four-day workshops in it every year, and I can't even imagine trying to rent someone else's space for those events. It just wouldn't be nearly as magical. I also have a monthly subscription, called *Studio Diaries*, and we do most of the filming for those in my studio. These videos give my larger global audience a chance to "hang out" in the studio as I paint, explore creative exercises, and chat with other artists.

In many ways, it feels like the heartbeat of my business lives inside my studio space.

Core Values

My core values are woven throughout my business in many different ways. For me, generosity, service, empowerment, and creative expression are really

at the core of everything I do and share, and the studio really supports that by providing a deeply nourishing space.

In the workshops, we go out of our way to make sure every student feels loved and taken care of the minute they walk in the door. We provide artfully presented organic food, love-filled goody bags, yoga classes, dance parties, massage therapy, live music, and plenty of one-on-one time with myself and my team. I want the experience to feel like a pampered creative retreat where anything is possible, and I'm happy to say that's the feedback we often receive.

Sweet Spot Style Living

I definitely had a sweet spot moment yesterday. We were out in the woods filming a video for *Studio Diaries*, which involved collecting inspiring items and creating a natural offering with them at the base of a tree. So there I am in a beautiful forest essentially building a fairy house, and I'm thinking, *now this is my version of success*!

So, yes, I agree with you completely, my sweet spot is that place where my passions, ethics, and abundance all meet. I'm deeply grateful to live in this place on most days.

Tips For Creatives

During a time of business transition, a friend of mine asked, "What feels like low-hanging fruit?" That always stuck with me. Asking yourself what feels exciting and accessible is a great way to check in about your next bold moves. This is not to say manifesting a creative business is easy, because it's definitely not. However, I'm a big believer in ease, following curiosity, and doing what feels truly interesting.

I'll also add that I don't think all creative passions are meant to be turned into businesses. Sometimes allowing your passion to remain an extracurricular activity is the best way to keep it alive.

Best Advice

I always love to remind folks that creative expression, doing what you love, and creating meaning in your life are all things that you *deserve*. They're not a luxury, they're actually crucial to your well-being.

Flora can be found online at florabowley.com
and on Instagram @florabowley.

Johanna Stark

I am: Graphic Designer, Illustrator
My home: Malmö, Sweden
My style: Playful. Homey. Eclectic.

Be thankful for what you've got. Try to be inspired by others instead of comparing yourself to them, even though it's hard at times. Maybe this is life advice, but it all blends together for me.

Johanna Stark is a freelance graphic designer and illustrator, living and working in Malmö, located in southern Sweden. She shares a small apartment with her boyfriend in the city, and that is also where her lovely work space is.

Your Creative Work

We love living in Sweden, but when it gets too dark and gloomy in the winter, we usually spend a couple months in some warm place and surf, so then I bring my work space to the tropics!

I love the combination of the two—the cooler climate in Sweden with its dramatically changing seasons, which I can follow with the big trees just outside my window, and the lush, green surroundings in places like Sri Lanka, where I can be outdoors and work.

I mostly work with patterns, usually drawing or painting by hand, and the inspiration often comes from the diversity in nature according to the seasons. Sometimes it can be pine

trees and small houses from the forest where I grew up, and another day it could be bold tropical leaves and exotic birds that inspire me.

From time to time I make screen prints, both on paper and fabric. I also make cards that I sell at some flower and gift shops. Currently, I am working on a new brand with a dear friend of mine, still a little secret project, but patterns and textiles will definitely be involved! In between the pattern making, I also do some graphic design jobs, like logotypes, usually with a hand-drawn approach, and once in a while I take on copywriting jobs. So every day is really quite different.

Last year I graduated from The Royal Danish Academy of Design in Copenhagen, but I feel that in this business every day is a constant learning experience in a very positive way.

Your Creative Work Space

My work space is super important for me; I am not the type that can easily sit in the middle of a busy coffee shop and work concentrating for hours. If I were

[in a coffee shop], I would probably just people watch and chitchat with the coffee shop owner and not get anything done. I need a calm surrounding, my pens and watercolors close to me, a bunch of magazines to cut out inspiring pictures from, and so on, in order to stay focused. Often, I also need my scanner to bring some hand-drawn sketch into the computer, or my printer to try something out in different scales, for example. All these things I have within arm's reach in my home office, which I am really grateful for.

Staying Organized

A couple of days a week, I work as a visual stylist and salesperson at a lovely lifestyle shop called Marimekko, so the rest of the week when I am in my home office, I feel really grateful to be there. Because I have limited time in my home studio, I'm often really eager to start working on my creative work.

Every Monday I create a schedule for the week to come, and I try not to be overoptimistic about how much stuff I can squeeze in. I'd rather be realistic. That way I get the satisfaction of finishing the stuff that I set out to do. This

helps keep me motivated and wanting to make new goals. I know that my best working hours are before lunch, so I tackle the harder tasks first, when I have the most energy.

Biggest Challenge

One of the biggest challenges is storing all my stuff: pens, papers, inspirations, etc. Every once in a while I take a couple hours of my day and organize all this stuff. I try to get rid of things I don't need, or I place them in our attic, in case I suddenly have the urge for some old sketches or something. The space where I have my desk used to be a quite unutilized space, since there was only a small, but long window frame. We had a sofa in front of it with just a little space in between. Then I came up with the idea of moving the sofa a little bit, making our living area just a little smaller, and using the whole area by the windows to make a work space.

Another challenge I've had is being able to relax after work since we are living in the same place I work. I've found that if I tidy up my desk after work every

day (which is really nice anyway), and decide to not work late evenings, then the space kind of transforms into a part of the living room after the workday.

Practical + Pretty

My boyfriend and I created the work table with just some wood we sawed and painted and some inexpensive table legs from IKEA. Once we painted everything (it was in two pieces) and were about to put it in place, we realized that we had the measurements wrong and one piece was too short. Luckily, we had one piece left that we could make the right size. We ended up not painting that one, since we found it pretty cool to have the table in two colors.

The leftover piece that was the wrong size I now use as a notice board. The filing cabinets are filled with all kinds of supplies that come in handy when you are in a creative mood: tape in different colors, strings, all kinds of glue, hard wire, colored paper, different kinds of paint, inspirational cards and brochures from all over the world, invoices, staplers, and stamps.

The metal piece on the wall (see photo on page 107) I found in our attic. It was left over from someone's renovation project, and I thought it would fit nicely on my wall. I used to have just a string I hung prints on, but this fits much better and looks nice as well. I enjoy thinking about how things can be used and not wasted.

Botanicals

Sometimes I feel like the plants are almost taking over, but I love my plants! The reason they are in my work space is because they have nowhere else to go in our small apartment. But I think they provide a nice feeling to the space, and plants do make the air cleaner. They also work almost as a meditation for me. Sometimes I take a break from whatever I am doing and pick some dead leaves off, give them a little water, or rearrange how they are placed. Since I was little I have enjoyed taking care of plants, and they are also a big source of inspiration in my work.

Best Advice

Work with what you have! It sounds simple, but it really is true. You don't have to buy the most expensive work desk ever or rent a super fancy office in order to stay creative. Just try to find what works for you. Really try to see the possibilities of what you have instead of what you don't have—I guess this applies to pretty much everything in life.

And don't forget the power of plants! Having something living in your work space that you have to take care of really can help clear your mind.

Every once in a while, do something in your work space that is just for fun. For example, if you like to draw, draw something that's not work related, but just fun for you! This helps to make your work space a place where you want to be.

Johanna can be found at johannastark.se
and on Instagram @johannastark.

Sue Henry

I am: Creative Director/Owner of Tulusa LLC
My home: Alexandria, Virginia
My style: Modern. Organic.

The people that I'm most attracted to in life are people who nurture, who love unconditionally, and who are still strong and solid. That is how my studio feels to me.

Artist Sue Henry opened her first home goods business after years of working as a ceramic artist building life-size (and larger) figurative work and fountains in California. After moving to the East Coast and experiencing a lack of space, she started bringing her work indoors. Sue now produces a personal line of original block-printed and embellished textiles for her shop, Tulusa.

Your Creative Work

I have a long history of being in the arts. With a BFA in ceramics and sculpture, I worked in clay for years making large-scale figurative work. When my boys were babies, working on that scale within our home, where my studio is, became much more difficult. I turned to carving linoleum blocks because it was less dusty and I could leave it for weeks at a time if I needed to. From there, I started to print on fabric. However, a new business opportunity arose, and I left it all behind. That was nearly eight years ago. In 2015, I pulled out a bin of prints and just started working on them. Soon I was up and running, and in November of 2015, Tulusa became a reality.

Tulusa is a textile design business that specializes in block printing and creating home goods and personal accessories. I like to keep my textiles light, bright, and pretty, with an end goal of providing well-made, beautiful products that my clients will cherish and love to give as gifts.

Creative Work Space

Having a home studio is really important because it allows me to get right into work as soon as I send my two boys off to school. Although it's in the garage, it was built as a modern space with tons of natural light. There is a glass garage door that gives me a full view of the garden and offers a sweet space to sit and take a break.

Inside we've built in storage and shelves, making it a space that is both functional and pretty. I've surrounded myself with the color of my textiles and plants, so it has become my own personal oasis and where I want to spend most of my time.

One of my favorite things is an old school drafting table that we bought for $50 from a business that was selling their older pieces. I use that drafting table daily. It's high enough and large enough for me to print large pieces of fabric, and it is the center point of the studio.

Staying Organized

Lists, lists, lists! While I like to work in an organic way, doing what I *feel* like doing on any given day, I know I need concrete systems to help me stay on track. Working this way, my business has grown rather quickly.

I have a cabinet that doubles as a dry erase board, and on that board I make a list of what needs to happen each week. Taking a step back from that, I look at each quarter and the goals that I've set.

I've started to do something that I never thought I would, which is to create spreadsheets for wholesale and retail sales and plug in everything before I start to build my product line for the new season. It gives me a great base to accomplish my goals.

These glass doors provide light to the studio and a connection to the rest of the house.

*Sue's converted garage studio opens up to a sunny patio, perfect
for taking an afternoon cocktail break.*

Biggest Challenge

It used to be space. Fortunately, we recently did a big studio upgrade. We got
rid of a couple of problem pieces that were taking up way too much room
in the space. Now we have new drawers and a cabinet that hold a lot of my
finished work. I can see that in a couple of years my space may be too small for
my business, but for now it's perfect.

Pretty + Practical

Drawers! They are very plain, yet highly functional and keep me organized.
I didn't love them until I added some beautiful handles that I found at
Anthropologie. They help to make my space a little more feminine. That set
of drawers also has a pretty wood top that I can work at, put a vase of flowers
on, or have my kids draw or do their homework there. I love that it's become a
multipurpose space where my people like to hang out, too.

Sweet Spot Style Living

Living in my sweet spot means having freedom to be at work any time of the
day or night. I love what I do, and being able to jump into my studio at the
crack of dawn or, more often than that, work into the wee hours of the night
helps to keep things going without missing out on family time.

Core Values

I am a pretty open person and like to think that I play well with others. I would say that my new space reflects that. It's open with its glass garage door and big side windows. It's also nurturing, full of plants and color. The people that I'm most attracted to in life are people who nurture, who love unconditionally, and who are still strong and solid. That is how my studio feels to me.

Style Tips

If you need new pieces of furniture for your space to function properly, I say bite the bullet and invest in your space. The best thing that I've done in my home in the past six years (since we built it) was to put my foot down and get rid of the pieces that weren't working for me. My space reflects who I am, and it still works for my family. It's now a space that is open and bright. It's perfect for keeping my creativity flowing.

Find Sue online at tulusa.com
and on Instagram @tulusa.goods.

Kyah Wilson

I am: Artist
My home: Dubbo, Australia
My style: Eclectic. Country. Rustic. A Hint of Jungalow and Hamptons.

Painting from my studio doesn't feel like work.

Kyah Wilson is an Australian contemporary artist. Having spent her childhood drawing and creating, she continued her passion for art with studies in fine art at Seaforth TAFE and the College of Fine Arts, Paddington. In lieu of completing her studies, Kyah traveled extensively, married, and had five children. Her passion for art was put on hold.

After a seventeen-year hiatus, her innate desire to create art was reignited when her family moved to a former dairy farm overlooking the plains of the Macquarie River in Dubbo. Inspired by the vast space and livestock grazing amongst the stillness and sunlight, she embraced her desire to produce art that resonates with her environment.

Kyah is inevitably drawn to Australian animals, having spent her childhood holidays at her family's sheep and cattle farm on the western Victorian coast. Animals are a reoccurring motif in her pieces and are illustrated to blend seamlessly with the weathered background.

Through her practice, she correlates the relationship of her quintessential Australian life, both past and current, epitomizing the intrinsic link between her life and art.

Your Creative Work

I am a contemporary Australian artist. I paint from a two-room studio situated in our paddock at the rear of our home in Dubbo, a regional town in Central Western New South Wales on the eastern side of Australia. It's about a five-hour drive from Sydney. It is a country-style home with a wraparound veranda with five acres of garden and paddocks. We overlook floodplains and the river that winds through the town.

I paint using mixed media, and often my subjects are inspired by my rural life and the farm animals that I see in my everyday life.

Your Creative Work Space

My work space is ever-evolving. The longer I'm here, the more I accumulate, and it is slowly becoming more homey. I enjoy spending time in my sunlit studio and painting room, as it is comfortable and I'm surrounded by things I love. I am also inspired to paint by the vast views I have of cattle grazing in the distance.

The Landscape

The colors of the Australian landscape form the basis of my work. The soft pastels of the sky, the earthy, neutral tones of the landscape, and the rustic feel of much-loved buildings of a bygone era.

Biggest Challenge

The biggest challenge was making my studio feel like home. My large white walls were cold and empty until I started hanging art and photos. I also brought in a lot of vintage wares and plants to make it come alive.

Pretty + Practical

I stay organized by having three long tables to keep my paints on according to medium, such as oils, acrylics, and aerosols. I also have a small canvas storage area and a room where I store and pack my finished pieces.

I occasionally clear each area and reorganize paints, canvases, and art. I move my homewares and furniture around and take photos to look at the areas from a different perspective.

Sweet Spot Style Living

Painting from my studio doesn't feel like work. My space is warm, peaceful, and inviting. My outlook is a rural landscape with amazing sunsets. I couldn't ask for anything better.

Core Values

My studio is filled with elements and items I love. I have no certain style. It is an eclectic mix of furniture and wares I've picked up randomly on my travels. If you buy only what you love and not stick to a certain style, you create your own [style]. Individuality is the key.

Sweet Spot Style Tip

It sounds cliché, but do what you love, be grateful, be consistent, be experimental, be you.

Kyah can be found at kyahwilson.com.au, on Instagram @kyahwilson_art, and on Facebook at Kyah Wilson Art.

Amira Rahim

I am: Artist, Business Owner, Creativity Advocate
My home: New Jersey
M style: Vibrant. Colorful. Uplifting.

*I try to remind myself that it's okay to enjoy where I am,
and to celebrate what fuels me in this moment, while fully
realizing that my sweet spot may look completely different
ten years from now.*

Your Creative Work

I'm a full-time artist based in New Jersey. I sell my artwork
to hundreds of collectors around the world. I also do a bit
of licensing and coach other artists. While in college, I
thought I was going to be a lawyer or a college professor,
yet today I'm a professional painter. This happened after
trying a few jobs out of college that I thought would be
the dream, but instead I didn't feel like I was using all of
my unique talents and gifts. As a painter and business
owner, I have to wear many hats that I find challenging and
rewarding. Each day is different, and as it turns out, I thrive
in a more free-flowing type of life instead of one of routine.

This winding path that once troubled me in my youth is
now one that I embrace. There's a level of uncertainty that
I face daily, not only as an artist, but also as a business
owner. Learning to embrace the unknown and operate
without an exact destination has made the last few years
exciting, empowering, and invigorating. Here are my top
three tips:

1. **Fall in love with your own path.** This is something that I had to embrace over the years. When I first took the leap to start painting consistently and eventually being a full-time artist, I remember feeling this strong sense of urgency. I was twenty-four, but you would have thought I was double that (although there's no wrong age to pursue your lifelong passion). But I remember being so caught up in the fact that everyone else was already doing the thing I finally realized I wanted to do. I felt like I needed to catch up. I wanted to skip the years of hard work and slugging in the trenches that I knew were ahead. But we know by now that there's no magic way to skip over that. Now, I look at my own place and feel a sense of ease. I still push hard to accomplish my goals, but the difference is now I am only in competition with myself. I think when you compare your yesterday to where you are now, that is the true measure . . . and the only measure we should be using to measure success and, ultimately, happiness.

2. **Nurture your intuition.** I can't stress this enough; my intuition is my greatest asset. I don't think it's a coincidence that my ability to use my intuition in my personal life strengthened after I started using intuition to guide my abstract canvases. The former was really called upon by the latter, and it's one of the many reasons why I feel so grateful to lead this creative life. A regular art practice really does spill into other facets of being, and I believe can make someone a better person. Maybe it's those long, quiet hours in the studio or the waves of emotion it takes to consistently push further artistically, but you get comfortable with being uncomfortable pretty quickly when you face a blank canvas every day. I find meditation, speaking with licensed coaches and therapists, and journaling really help with tapping into what *I really need for my soul*, not just what I *think* I want based on what the outside world is telling me.

3. **Be passionately in love with your process.** Whatever that *thing* is that you do, if you don't love the work, no matter how much success or fame you get from it, you won't want to get out of bed in the morning. Art has been the one constant in my life. When I was a schoolteacher for a few years out of college, I turned to my art as a form of meditation and

gratitude. When I was a kid, I turned to my art and would draw places I wanted to live in. Today, my art still keeps me grounded and allows me to tap into my inner child. Even though the business side of things can be stressful at times, I am always excited to hit my studio. No matter what's going on around me, I still feel *good* about the work and the process of making art, and I feel like that keeps me grounded. Whether I'm painting in a high-rise apartment in Dubai, in an artist commune in Mexico, or sitting on the rocks by the sea off the coast of Italy, it's all the same for me. I'm in love with the process of making art, and it is how I learned to stay present in this fast-paced world.

You can find Amira online at amirarahim.com
or hanging out on Instagram @amirarahimart.

the home office

Create the Style You Crave While Working from Home

I have several creative work spaces in my home, it's true. In the summer, you will often find me on my front porch. I've also been known to cuddle up in one of our big, comfy chairs scattered around the house. Lately, I've also taken to standing up at the kitchen bar (it's good for your back). I also have a study nook downstairs where I work on my vision books and take client calls. But when it comes to writing my books and running the day-to-day of my online business, this is my favorite place to work.

You might be surprised to learn that my office is in my bedroom, especially considering I have an office downstairs. I recently updated this room by adding wallpaper by Hygge and West (designed by Oh Joy!; see page 31 for her story) to one wall. The rest of the room is painted white, which is great for clarity. The combination of this modern boho paper with the crisp white walls felt so good that it inspired me to create my work space here.

When creating your own home office, don't feel that it has to be in a traditional space. As you'll see in this chapter, your office can be in your bedroom, at the top of your stairs, in a foyer, or as part of your living area. The main thing is to ensure that the design and area beckon you to do your best work.

For my bedroom office, I combined a modern desk with a vintage rug and chair to create an eclectic look. Architect desk by Ikea. Rug from Candle in the Night, lamp from Target, vintage chair purchased at a neighbor's tag sale for $10.

Nazanin Pouresmaili

I am: Bartender, Designer
My home: Oslo, Norway
My style: Eclectic. Thrift/Vintage with a Bohemian Twist.

I like to redesign and reuse whatever I can.

Your Creative Work Space

It was important to me to create a work space that's not only useful, but also looks great. Sometimes I sit on the sofa across the room when I am in a creative process instead of sitting at the desk. Having a nice eclectic work space as a view can sometimes give you the inspiration and energy that you need. The desk itself is teak. I found it at a flea market. It needed some love, so I put a coat of color and white pigmented oil on it. I love how it turned out.

The hanging board on the wall is actually an old destroyed clothing drying rack. Since I like to redesign and reuse whatever I can, it ended up on the wall. When I'm in a creative process, it can be used to hang up mood boards and inspiration. The rest of the time it's just for decoration.

I'm falling more and more in love with green plants, and the palm tree is both beautiful and relaxing. It's also easy to move if I need the space. The library lamp and the clutch are also second hand. The clutch went from being a *party purse* to being a decorative piece that hides important papers.

Biggest Challenge

Since I have my work space in the living room, which is kind of small, I had to find a solution that worked in

harmony with the rest of the room. I wanted to have it looking clean and tidy, but at the same time functional and practical.

Style Tips

Most important of all: lighting. Bad lighting equals a bad work environment, so invest in a good lamp.

Nazanin can be found online at nazanin-design.com
and on Instagram @bynazanin.

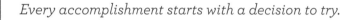

Cara Paige

I am: Founder of Cover Paige Creative
My home: Baltimore, Maryland
My style: Eclectic. Lux. Boho.

Every accomplishment starts with a decision to try.

Cara Paige is the founder and creative director of *Cover Paige Creative*. For the past fifteen years, she's shared her talent in marketing and design, partnering with national brands, nonprofits, and start-ups, and even debuted her marketing acumen at the White House. She's honed her skills to become an expert, teaching companies how to market and design the businesses they love.

Your Creative Work

Cover Paige Creative is an interior design, event production, styling, and experiential marketing agency. As creative director, I help individuals and brands—from small shops all the way to some of the world's most notable companies—tell their story by creating awe-inspiring experiences, atmospheres, and interior designs to connect them with their customers.

Your Creative Work space

I absolutely need to work in a space that is, first and foremost, neat and organized. I also want it to have a great aesthetic that inspires me to do my best work. I love the clean lines and modern design of my work space. I went with a classic black-and-white palette for this space so that

I can change my *it* color of the season whenever the mood strikes. I like being able to switch design elements when I'm ready for a change.

Biggest Challenge

The biggest challenge in my current home office is not being able to make any structural or permanent changes to the space. I've been able to camouflage it by creating an amazing black-and-white bold striped accent wall and starburst mirror that I love. It's an immediate eye-catcher and focal point in the space that kinda hides all the other less interesting elements. It truly carries the room. I also made sure that the rest of the design throughout the office is sleek with simple lines, which adds to the modern feel of the space. My intention is to create a minimalistic, clean, and lux space.

Pretty + Practical

I keep a variety of work systems all around my office to help me stay organized. I definitely love the pretty, but practical is right up there, too. First and foremost are my super organized bookshelves with boxes that literally have a place for everything . . . and I mean everything. I also have a credenza that stretches the length of my office. It hides all my cords, office items, tchotchkes, client files, books, etc.

In addition, I have storage folders for most of the paperwork, especially for recurring client files, printouts, and projects. When everything has a place, I'm able to keep the productivity rolling along.

Core Values

At my very core, I believe in using my strengths and talents to work hard and produce excellent work to the best of my abilities. I try to be thorough and efficient in all that I do, always putting my best foot forward and giving 110 percent to every project.

Design Tips

Feature your personal artwork, memories, and visual inspirations that truly speak to you. For example, I frame vintage scarves, Instagram photos, and handwritten notes from friends and clients to add a personal touch.

Don't worry about trying to find or use traditional office furniture. Try using an old toy chest that can be converted into a place to hold your files, a china cabinet as a bookshelf, or an out-of-use dining room table that can be converted into an amazing and unique desk.

Using greenery or flowers always brings life to a space. Don't have a green thumb or time to care for a plant every day? Treat yourself to a nice bouquet of flowers every other week; it truly makes all the difference.

You can find Cara online at coverpaigecreative.com, on Instagram @CvrPaige, and on Facebook at CoverPaigeCreative.

Stasia Savasuk

I am: Founder of Stasia's Style School
My home: Brattleboro, Vermont
My style: Vibrant. Soul-Filled. True.

What I love BEST about my creative work space is that it is a clear reflection of my values.

Stasia Savasuk is a dear friend and neighbor. She's the founder of Stasia's Style School and a personal stylist—with a twist! Her unconventional-transformation-motivational approach to style leads women of all ages and stages on an intuitive journey of letting go, knowing what they know, and embracing a life filled with confidence, courage, and inside–out congruency. Stasia knows that changing your pants will change your life, and she has ushered hundreds of women away from years of body-shaming, negative self-talk, and muffin-top jeans to a place of body acceptance and pants that fit to flatter—thank you very much. Stasia can be seen frolicking in the woods of Vermont with her two kids, wearing a skirt, big earrings, red lipstick, and a friendly smile.

Your Creative Work

Though I work as a personal stylist today, I would have burst out laughing at such a preposterous proposition just five years ago! I broke up with style in my twenties and had convinced myself that being stylish and eco-conscious were mutually exclusive paths. I didn't think I had the body or the money to wear cute clothes. I held tight to the belief that style was petty and superficial, and, anyway, it's what's on the inside that matters.

When my daughter was born in 2007 with a number of medical needs, I became a stay-at-home mama. I would wander the streets of my little town and pop into the neighborhood thrift shop almost daily. I would buy things. Cute things that only cost $4. I experimented and tried every color, cut, and style that was out there. I learned that size doesn't matter, shape does. I learned that certain colors set my soul ablaze, while others downright deflated me. I discovered that some clothes connected me to parts of my soul I had long forgotten, like my strength, bravery, and even my voice. I came to see that when I wore the *right* clothes, I was kinder, more vibrant, more *alive*.

Though I believed these lessons to be true for me, I didn't think they applied to my daughter, who at age two started trending toward boy's clothes. I figured it was just a phase. By the time she was three, I could hardly get her into a dress, though you better believe I tried. By age five, it was a full-on assault against anything girly. And then when she was six, she asked me to buy her a shirt and necktie during a shopping trip to our local thrift shop. I wanted to say no, but I said yes, with every intention of the combo disappearing!

When we got home, my daughter couldn't wait to try on her shirt and necktie. I busied myself with work. And then out of the corner of my eye, I watched her look in the mirror and literally take her own breath away. Moments later, she ran across the living room and said, "Mama Mama, look how fast I can run!" And then she jumped high into the air and said, "Mama, Mama, look how much higher I can jump when I'm wearing a shirt and tie!"

That was it. She could *run faster* and *jump higher* when she was wearing clothes on the outside that matched who she was on the inside.

In that moment, belief systems crumbled, and I realized I was caught in a box that said *this* is what a girl is supposed to look like. Then I thought about *all* the boxes we find ourselves caught in. There are boxes for all the shapes, all the sizes, all the ages, all the roles. And they are preventing humans all over the world from showing up authentically, because breaking out of that box is almost impossible.

Paradigms shifted for me that day, and in that moment I realized that *this* was my vocation.

Staying Organized

To stay focused and organized, it's a must for me to work in my creative work space, because otherwise the mess of the house distracts me and I find myself sweeping, doing dishes, and cleaning toilets! And that is one sure way to dampen productivity.

I also don't allow any distractions into my space, like TV or music . . . or my kids! And, if I can help it, my Facebook newsfeed.

It's important for me to keep my work space tidy, uncluttered, and filled only with things that make my heart happy. It is *my* space, and the whole family knows not to mess with mama's space. The rest of the house can be in complete disarray, but my space is always an oasis of clarity, cleanliness, and creative inspiration.

Biggest Challenge

My biggest home office challenge until rather recently was that I didn't have a home office. Before I had my own space, I was completely disorganized. I had piles of things all around the house, and it made me (and my family) batty.

I live in a very small home (1,200 square feet), so I disqualified myself from ever having a home office because there was no four-walled space for me to call my own. Once my creative venture turned from hobby to business, the need for me to have my own space became obvious to the whole family. We got creative, and I claimed an upstairs hallway nook as my own. Though my home office may appear small to some, to me it feels expansive and lavish.

Pretty + Practical

Since my home office is very small, I only bring in pieces that suit my aesthetic in their charm and functionality.

My vintage gold basket holds sweet handwritten note cards from past clients. My vintage purse holds all my business receipts. My vintage recipe box holds my business cards. My vintage sewing box holds office necessities, like pens, pushpins, and postage stamps.

I had a contractor build a custom shelving unit so that I could have ready access to resources and literature without having to trek downstairs to the family bookshelf. I chose a desk with drawers so that my business/ accounting materials could be hidden, yet organized.

I have a vision board (gifted to me from Desha!) so that I can stay focused on my dreams, without overwhelming myself with Post-it notes and long-term goal reminders. Inspired by my photographer's vision, I've even used my electric cord as a design feature on the leg of my desk. I love it!

My space does just what it has been created to do: inspire, motivate, excite, and be a place of calm and clarity when I need it.

Core Values

What I love *best* about my creative work space is that it is a clear reflection of my values. Two things I value most are supporting women in their creative entrepreneurial ventures, either locally or globally, and upcycling/recycling things that are already in planetary circulation.

Most of the art in my office was created by artists I love and admire (many of whom are Stasia's Style School alums!). Each handmade piece reminds me that I am both supported by and supportive of women who are flexing their brave muscles by releasing their creative prowess into the world.

I also love finding vintage treasures from thrift stores and reimagining how I might use them in my space in a way that is both functional *and* pretty.

Best Advice

I have found that in this world of pretty things, it is of supreme importance to go beyond the pretty and fill your space with things that are a reflection of *you*.

Your values. Your quirks. Your charm.

In other words, I believe that when you walk into a creative's work space, you should get a glimpse into their creative soul. I prefer an eclectic mix of box-store pretties alongside found trophies and trinkets from thrift shops, sidewalk piles, and yard sales. We, as creatives, are not replicable, nor should our creative space be.

When I work with clients as a style coach, I always start with the question, "Who are you way down deep inside your soul?" I'm not looking to know what roles you play in life. I'm looking to know what words you would use to describe your soul fire.

Our work as creatives is a composite of our truest nature *and* our values, so I think it's important to consider both when designing *our* creative work space.

Eccentricity takes time! Don't rush the process.

Tips for Creatives

Oh, this is a tricky one! I sometimes wonder if I found my sweet spot, or if it found me. I never thought I would someday become an entrepreneur, and I certainly *never* expected I would become a personal stylist, helping women

break out of old belief systems, flex their brave muscles, and show up in a way that reflects their soul fire on the outside!

But my story became my truth. It was what propelled me. I had to decide whether or not to follow that propulsion or maintain my day job. I am a linear thinker. A planner. I do not take uncalculated risks. But there came a time when I had to choose between saying yes to a job that promised me more money than I could ever dream of or saying yes to my soul's work, even though it might not make me a single penny. I chose my soul's work, and I am forever grateful for that lapse in qualified judgment!

Find Stasia online at stasiasavasuk.com, at stasiasstyleschool.com, and on Instagram @stasiasavasuk.

Liz Kamarul

I am: Stylist, Home Stager, Traveler
My home: Portland, Oregon
My style: Eclectic. Boho. Jungle.

I love that in my own home I never have to question whether someone will like what I do, because I really don't care.

Liz Kamarul has been obsessed with design her whole life. Always rearranging, redecorating, and trying new things. She went to school for design, graduated, and then lived in several different cities across the United States. She also spent some time in Australia, where she met her Aussie husband, Tim. For the past three years, she has been living in Portland, Oregon, and working as a home stager. In her free time, she works on the new home they purchased a little over a year ago. By the time this book comes out, Liz and her husband will have quit their jobs to spend the summer living in an RV and touring the states. Liz says, "I am looking for new adventure, a new place to live, and a fresh start."

Your Creative Work

My job as a home stager is very different from designing my own space. When I meet with a client at their home, I'm looking at how to present their space in a way that will appeal to as many different individual style preferences as possible. That means a lot of neutral color choices and minimal design. I like to accentuate the home and its features, since at the end of the day that is what we are trying to sell versus the decor.

Now, my own space is just the opposite. I'm always trying to make my house as interesting and unique as possible by choosing things many people would shy away from, like black ceilings or crazy patterned couches from the '60s/'70s. I love that in my own home I never have to question whether someone will like what I do, because I really don't care ... other than my husband, who actually has the exact opposite design preference than I do. But he is so supportive and kind. He knows that this means everything to me and gives me free rein to do what I want!

Biggest Challenge

Tim and I share the office, and the most difficult thing about it has been trying to figure out where it should be. This home never really had an office space at all, so originally we were going to turn the mudroom in the back of our home into an office.

Once we completed renovations of that area, we realized that because it's west facing and we added glass French doors, that it wouldn't be the best spot for computers because it gets so bright and hot in the afternoon. So we turned that into our dining room and made what was intended to be the dining room into the work space. That ended up being a great choice because it's more open to the rest of the house and doesn't feel like you're shut away in seclusion.

Liz loves her space to evolve. By nature she's a "maximalist" when it comes to design, but here we get a glimpse of her minimalist side.

Style Tips

A work space can be so many different things depending on how you function with your surroundings, but for us it was important to have artwork that was inspiring, textiles, plants, and good lighting.

You can find Liz online at lizkamarul.com and on Instagram @liz_kamarul.

Liz hand-painted this gorgeous mural, shown on left, adding a focal point and originality to the space.

Sarah Bennett

I am: Owner of House Fly Co., Vintage Curator, Lighthearted Card Maker, Virtual Assistant
My home: Corvallis, Oregon
My style: Happy. Colorful. Vintage. Bohemian.

My current creative work space reflects my belief that you do what you can with what you have!

Sarah Bennett is a talented artist, graphic designer, and vintage shop owner with a keen eye for design. She started off as a client, and now she helps me run my business!

Your Creative Work

I went to college for public relations and art not knowing exactly what I wanted to do. I went through my twenties working jobs just to pay the bills and felt quite empty inside. I was in a cycle of switching jobs almost every year, which was mentally and emotionally exhausting.

When I hit my midtwenties, I took the train across the country with my sister and enrolled in a yoga teaching program to take time out and look within. It was healing and ultimately the beginning of my quest to pursue doing creative work that I love. I found myself coming back to the natural interests I had as a little girl.

I was always putting together outfits, decorating the house, and coming up with innovative designs; it's how I played. I am lucky to have a husband who has stuck beside me through the days I felt lost. He is the one who finally said,

"Sarah, why don't you just do what makes you happy." A big fat *duh* really, but I needed to hear that apparently to move forward!

I started my online vintage and card shop in August of 2016. I had dreamed of having my own online shop for a long time and finally made that dream a reality. I invested in getting one-on-one guidance [with Desha]. Having that accountability piece and someone to understand my goals and vision was instrumental in the process of creating my shop.

When it came down to figuring out my product, I just observed how I was spending my free time. I have always been a "thrifter" and get such a thrill out of hunting for beautiful unique pieces to wear, so it seemed natural to hone in on this and make something of it.

In addition to my love of hunting for vintage gems, I get great joy out of making card designs. I stumbled upon graphic design in 2014 and taught myself how to use Illustrator and just loved it.

Before I knew it, I was getting requests left and right to create wedding invites, shower invites, Christmas and business cards. I wove in my design love with my vintage clothes, and House Fly Co. was born. This is really the beginning of creative entrepreneurship for me, but I'm loving every minute of this path and cannot wait to see how it evolves.

Your Creative Work Space

My current creative space is rather small. My husband and I moved from a three-bedroom home into a 600-square-foot apartment, which was a major space change for us! I have had to get creative and use what I have to make the space work for me. It's been a creative challenge, but I have definitely claimed it as my own.

I have an old steel work desk with a minty-colored surface and lots of room to spread out on. My desk is situated between two windows, and I get lots of natural light, which keeps my energy up!

I live in the country, so I have a view of the trees. Having a pretty view is always a plus for creative work. I also decorated my creative nook with things that lift me up and reflect who I am. I love a mix of vintage and earthy bohemian pieces, and plants are a must in my creative work space. Color-wise, I gravitate toward lighter palettes for my work space.

Staying Organized

I found a cute midcentury dresser that I use to store my vintage clothes and cards and art supplies. I also have a clothes rack nearby so I can see the pretty clothes I collect; it makes me happy to see the vintage patterns and colors.

Biggest Challenge

The biggest challenges are lack of storage, small space, and that it is a rental. My husband helped me build three-tier corner shelves by my desk, which have been a great help with organization and storage. We used recycled materials to make the shelves, so the cost was minimal. I found a dresser for $30 on craigslist that fits perfectly in the space, and that's been a huge help with storage. I also have a small file cabinet I thrifted and painted to help me stay organized.

To make my space brighter and appear larger to my eye, I purchased a light hemp woven rug. Having that lighter color on the ground makes it feel larger and also sections off my space from the kitchen. I layered a smaller vintage rug on top to bring in more color.

Sweet Spot Style Living

Living in my sweet spot means waking up and being excited to work! It means doing creative work I love from home and making good money doing it. It means being my own boss and enjoying flexibility in my day-to-day schedule.

Pretty + Practical

I use storage to help my space stay pretty and practical. Also, it was important to find a desk that is large enough for me to spread out and not feel restricted.

I use the walls as storage by hanging a file rack from Ikea and a small hexagon bulletin board to tack notes and inspirational sayings onto.

Style Tips

If you're in an open living space, you could also create a movable wall and paint it with chalkboard paint or paint a mural or color that excites you.

Think of an awkward space as a fun design challenge. Play around with the arrangement and notice what feels best for you.

Best Advice

I have found that the creative path is the healing path. It takes a great deal of courage and vulnerability to do creative work. Which is why designing a space that completely describes your essence and lures you in to create and share more with the world is incredibly important. Enjoy the process; we're creatives after all, and we know how to have fun!

Find Sarah on Instagram
@sarahsoleil11.

Sara Banner

I am: Fiber Artist
My home: New Cumberland, Pennsylvania
My style: Modern. Eclectic. Simplicity.

I find that my creativity thrives when my work space is clean and organized.

Your Creative Work Space

I am a self-taught fiber artist with a concentration in macramé and weaving. I started creating macramé plant hangers and wall hangings for my own home in early 2016 and quickly realized that I wanted to share my work with others. Since that time, my work has been constantly evolving as I incorporate new techniques and materials. I'm excited to spend the next year sharing my passion through teaching and also continuing to learn myself. I just enrolled in a pottery course, and I can't wait to try to weave ceramics into my hangings!

Sweet Spot Style Living

Living in my sweet spot means that my home is a reflection of my family and a source of creative inspiration. As a family, we to try to foster simplicity in our home and our life. This decision has really helped me to hear my own voice when it comes to decorating our space.

Sara Banner's DIY DESK

I found the desk on craigslist for $10 and decided to strip off the damaged original finish and then apply a clear wax to preserve the natural quality of the wood. I like the traditional lines of the desk, but to fit my style it needed a little bit of a bohemian edge. It was a time-consuming process, but I felt like this was the perfect solution. The white porcelain knobs were left over from some cabinets we removed from our kitchen.

My mother painted the portrait that's over my desk when she was in high school. It is loosely based on my aunt, my mom's sister Kay. It hung in my grandmother's home for as long as I can remember, and I love seeing it in our home.

I found the small original primitive painting at a local antique store for less than $20, with the frame and all! I always try to buy original art whenever I can. Vintage stores are a great resource for this in our area.

The piece that's hanging from the desk is one of my macramé pieces that was waiting to be packed up for a client.

Biggest Challenge

Whenever you are committed to buying vintage or secondhand pieces, it can always take a bit longer than if you just went out to a store to purchase the things that you want. I searched craigslist for quite a while until I was able to find a solid wood desk with good lines for a reasonable price. Thankfully, my brother-in-law was visiting that week with his truck! After getting it home, it took many weeks to strip and refinish the desk.

After that, I knew that I wanted to contrast the traditional lines of the desk with a modern light fixture. Luckily, I was able to snag the blue corded fixture for a great price during a sale at Anthropologie, and the oversize bulb is from Ikea. I love the pop of bright blue in the otherwise neutral space.

Staying Organized

I love a desk with a drawer so that you can keep the top of your work space clutter-free. I work from my home and find that my creativity thrives when

*Here's a snapshot of Sara's other work space, where she creates
her one-of-a-kind macramé pieces.*

my work space is clean and organized. Admittedly, I also have a giant wall calendar in a different space that I use to keep track of all of my projects and commitments. Thank goodness for that giant calendar!

Find Sara Banner online at theforestfern.com
and on Instagram @the_forestfern.

creative work spaces for groups

Have you ever dreamed of having your own beautiful work space where you could create, but also share your space with other like-minded folks, perhaps offering workshops or retreats? In this section, you'll meet a couple of savvy biz ladies who have created multiuse spaces to accommodate their big visions.

The Bananaland, our next featured story, is used for office space, as well as for large workshops and events.

Marcella Kovac

I am: Founder of The Bananaland
My home: Bridgeport, Connecticut
My style: Mod. Funky. Eclectic. Retro. '70s Travel-Inspired.

My work space is an extension of who I am.

Marcella's obvious love of design and marketing has been undeniably influenced by her not-so-subtle wanderlust. A passion for experiencing new places and meeting new people, complemented by a deep appreciation for international art and commercial design, has resulted in a spin on the agency that mirrors top-notch hospitality, innovative thinking, and a memorable "stay." More often than not, you'll find her at the front desk of The Bananaland, charming clients with her genuine enthusiasm for delivering uniquely creative solutions or going on about her favorite travel destination of all: Bridgeport.

Your Creative Work

Pretty much since age three, with puppets and crayons, I enjoyed being creative. It took quite a few more years to learn that I could make a career out of it! During college, I was introduced to top-notch graphic designers including Stefan Sagmeister, Paula Sahre, and Jessica Helfand (still my heroes, plus many more). That's when it hit me: I wanted to establish a boutique creative business. My dream came true with the formation of The Bananaland! We offer branding, design, development, consulting, and social media services.

The Bananaland team consists of Marcella, her sister Laurie Kovac (art director), and Jordan Rabidou, a partner and technical lead.

I discovered your space when I attended the Monarch Workshop, a creative workshop for women. Can you talk about how this space is used beyond your design biz?
I love that our space makes people feel good and inspires other creatives. Beyond our office use, we often rent the space off-hours or on weekends to photographers and videographers. Plus, we host events like Monarch Workshop and Design Night Out, art shows, and, of course, the occasional just-for-fun party!

I *love* your studio, it's so *fun*! How does the space and decor reflect who you are as a brand and person?
It's lighthearted, full of interesting oddities, professional but not too serious. Pretty much exactly who I am! Our work is something we enjoy wholeheartedly, and I think our space really reflects that.

How important is your creative work space? What impact does it have on your business and life?

It's *so* important. My environment impacts me to the core. Plus, I want our clients to feel warm, welcome, and comfortable when we meet with them. The thoughtful touches are just as much for us as they are for the people who visit.

I see a yellow bike and a basketball hoop . . . are these props, or do you play around on them for real?

We sure do! It's essential for us to take breaks and reinvigorate. Play is something that not only relaxes us, but often guides our inspiration or our next big idea. Sometimes we brainstorm while shooting hoops!

Biggest Challenge

We are lucky not to have many challenges. The building is old and has soaring ceilings, which we love, but in the dead of summer it can get pretty steamy, and in the winter it can be chilly. Some don't like the fact that it's a three-flight walk-up, but it keeps us bananas in shape!

Pretty + Practical

We have a couple of filing cabinets to store paperwork, but most of our items are digital, so that reduces the need for tons of storage. We take turns (weekly) keeping the space neat and tidy. Every month, all three of us take an hour or so to do a deeper clean, organize, consolidate. We've integrated it into our routine.

Sweet Spot Style Living

I couldn't be more happy, proud, and fulfilled. I also have a unique sweet spot within a sweet spot! What makes our office space even more special is that it is located in a city that I care very much about. My community is like my family, and we are all supportive of one another's endeavors. I'm involved in a variety of projects for the city that are meaningful to me. I also live in Bridgeport, so it's largely about the lifestyle. I ride my bike to work, take long walks at Seaside Park next to my house, grab a bite with friends downtown. My sweet spot is all around me!

Core Values

My work space is an extension of who I am. I value friendship, community, urban living, thoughtfulness, details, quirks, weirdness, travel, cleverness,

collaboration, and fun. I do feel all those qualities come across within the space and in its energy.

What's up with all the bananas?

Well, it was first born from the concept that the best ideas are often *out of the box*, slightly off-kilter, bonkers, or *bananas*! Now, The Bananaland represents a place where it's always crazy, beautiful, and where your brand goes to get a tan.

In other words, it reflects both our dedication to our work and to our client services. One thing that sets us apart is that we treat each project and client with the utmost care. The '70s airline and tropical travel theme play into the hospitality side of our company, in true banana fashion! You sit back and enjoy a banana daiquiri, while we take care of the rest.

Find Marcella online at thebananaland.com
and on Instragam @bananalady.

Jessica Serra Huizenga

I am: Confetti Artist, Creative Dreamer, Romance Author, Sugar-Free Chef
My home: Wallingford, Connecticut
My style: Simple. Colorful. Fun.

My core business value centers around celebrating happiness, and I like to think my studio definitely reflects that.

Who makes a living making custom confetti? Jessica does! Just like Marcella from The Bananaland, I met Jessica at my first Monarch Workshop (a very cool creative workshop). Jessica is a multi-passionate lady boss. She's a romance author, sugar-free chef, workshop hostess extraordinaire and confetti artist. I mean, seriously, she makes a living making confetti. How cool is that?

Your Creative Work

Confetti ... it's like the quintessential symbol for celebrations, right? It's colorful and whimsical and fun and magical, everything you generally want a party to be. So why not really make it something special?

Well that's what I thought when I decided to start The Confetti Bar. I literally woke up one day and told my husband I wanted to open a confetti shop, and that's how this all began.

You have more than 30k followers on Instagram; mind sharing how that happened?

From the very beginning I was very lucky that we had a lot of organic social media growth. Bloggers especially responded really well to our entire business and concept, so we got to collaborate and work with a lot of awesome people and our following just naturally grew from there.

To keep this momentum, I've also become very aware of having a cohesive aesthetic when it comes to my feed. I want everyone who visits my profile to immediately get a sense of our vibe and brand, so I make sure that everything I post fits in line with that. It helps that it is 100 percent my style.

As a multi-passionate lady boss, how have you consciously created a work space that facilitates creativity for yourself and others?

Clearly I have a lot of interests, but it helps that they are all very much a part of who I am and what I love, so creating a cohesive space to house it all comes pretty naturally.

Since my current studio is mainly Confetti Land HQ, though, it can be a little bit of a struggle when I want to switch gears and work on another project. I've found that having separate spaces sort of helps with that. For example, while I do take photos and store my novels at the studio, when it comes time to actually write, I typically use my desk in my bedroom at home. That way my brain sort of knows how to switch gears based on the space I'm in, because when I'm at the studio it's hard not to think about confetti!

How does being in your current studio help you create the work you were meant to do?

Having a dedicated space for confetti making definitely makes me more productive, and it allows me to focus on my craft in a way that feels natural and inspiring. I started and built this business from the most visually uninspiring space, our basement, so I don't necessarily believe in letting your physical space hold you back, but once we moved into the studio, it was like the stars aligned and everything finally came together in a way that really let me explore the full potential of the brand. It allows me to exercise my creativity in a bigger way.

Your Creative Work Space

Because my business is so visual, I think having a space that is a physical representation of that has become essential, not just from an organizational standpoint, but from an inspirational one as well. It feels good when you're in a space that constantly reflects a positive vibe.

Core Values

My core business value centers around celebrating happiness, and I like to think my studio definitely reflects that. From the giant corkboard filled with photos and cards to the confetti-covered floors, it's kind of hard *not* to be happy when you're in Confetti Land!

Sweet Spot Style Living

Living in my sweet spot means being happy with whatever I'm doing and wherever I am for that moment. What makes me happy might grow, evolve, and change, but I always want to try new creative ventures and learn from all sorts of experiences and just be excited to see where life takes me.

Dream Job As A Kid

While I didn't really ever have a specific dream job as a child, I distinctly remember saying I wanted to do something unique. Filmmaking was always a passion as a kid/teenager, since my brother and I and our friends would use my dad's old video camera to make all kinds of crazy movies.

Tips For Creatives

Since happiness is something I'm very much all about, here are my five basic tips for creating happiness:

1. Be nice.

2. Stay committed.

3. Practice balance.

4. Keep true to you.

5. Take things one step at a time.

Find Jessica online at theconfettibar.com and on Instagram @theconfettibar.

Brittney Borjeson

I am: Owner of Evoke the Spirit
My home: Sayulita + San Miguel de Allende, Mexico
My style: Raw. Modern, Traditional.

Life and time make the most beautiful things.

Evoke the Spirit started as a small shop in Sayulita, Mexico. Together with Wiraxia artisans, ex-pat Brittney Borjeson began designing a line of jewelry using traditional methods to create something new. Collaborations grew to encompass many of Mexico's indigenous and local artists. Now the collections include textiles, ceramics, cow skulls (made of bone and porcelain), and jewelry. Evoke the Spirit can now be found in Sayulita, San Miguel de Allende, and online.

Your Creative Work

I started Evoke the Spirit as an experiment. I wanted a space to be creative and work with the highly skilled indigenous artisans I was seeing all over Mexico.

Your Creative Work Space

Our studio/shop is everything. It determines how we work, how we feel when we work, and, ultimately, what the work becomes.

Biggest Challenge

I've found many challenges working with another culture. The biggest is breaking down my own expectations.

Core Values

I believe in rawness. Not just materials, but in life. It's why I live in Mexico. It's why I collaborate with indigenous culture. It's why I only work with materials that are alive, or that were made by life.

Style Tips

Style with nature as often as possible.

You can find Brittney at evokethespirit.com
or on Instagram @evokethespirit.

Vienda Maria, featured in the following Gypsetter section, works wherever there's WiFi.

work from anywhere, anytime

In The Kitchen, On The Floor, In Bed

After seeing some of the gorgeous spaces in this book so far (especially those bigger studios!), you might feel that having your own sweet spot space is a wee bit out of reach. Please don't. Let those stories inspire you, and if that's something you crave, put it on your list to work toward. Until then, don't forget that you can make any nook or cranny a perfectly sweet spot to work in.

Even though I have multiple places to work in my house, I often end up working from bed. I mean, why not? In this section, we'll see how Nichol Naranjo has created a lovely spot in what she calls the *banquette area*. If you don't have a dedicated spot in your home, take note. If you have room for a table, there's hope.

Then we'll hear from photographer Caroline White, who defines a new generation of virtual biz ladies. Learn why she's getting out of the house to find her sweet spot work space.

Nichol Naranjo

I am: Interior Designer
My home: Albuquerque, New Mexico
My style: Bohemian. Eclectic. Beachy.

Not having a dedicated office requires a little creativity, organization, and a well-thought-out space.

Your Creative Work

My love for interior styling began when I was about five years old. My mother gave me creative freedom in my bedroom my entire childhood, even through the dreaded teen years. I took great pride in each design and constantly redesigned my small bedroom, even as a young girl. I began to dabble in my own home as an adult from the get-go, as well as in the homes of others, and quickly realized that designing a home is something I am very passionate about. I want myself, my family, as well as everyone else around me to have a beautiful escape from the sometimes harsh realities of life the moment they walk into their homes.

Sweet Spot Style Living

Living and working in my sweet spot means I am creating a home that my entire family not only loves, but feels connected to. I aim to do the same with any home I help style/design. I think a home should inspire the person(s) that it houses. As soon as I see someone get excited and feel connected to a space I design, it confirms I am doing what I am supposed to be doing. It's important to me that my home—and any home I design—constantly evolves, just as we do.

Your Creative Work Space

Not having a dedicated office requires a little creativity, organization, and a well-thought-out space. When I designed my banquette area, I was determined to incorporate all of those things. This nook is in a corner in our living area that used to house a piano and was honestly wasted space.

I wanted a space that could act as a corner for homework, poker nights, my office, and an overflow dining area when having parties. With all of those things in mind, I knew I needed adequate work space (and, yes, the built-in bench doubles as a work space), seating, lighting, and it had to be a place that looked beautiful and inspiring as well.

I not only get to enjoy the natural light that pours in from the window, but I also had overhead lighting installed and put it on a dimmer. I also knew

the area needed an adequate number of electrical outlets for laptops, phone chargers, glue guns, and anything else that might require electricity.

With that in mind, we hid a couple of power strips underneath the custom-built benches that I designed. Directly across the room from my work space is a China hutch that houses the items I need when it's time to get to work: my laptop, notebooks, pens/markers/pencils, rug samples, and a basket of "extras" that come in handy. All of my supplies are hidden behind closed doors on the bottom cabinet of the China hutch and are easily accessible. I really enjoy this hardworking space and so does my family!

Find Nichol online at nicholnaranjo.com
and on Instagram @nicholnaranjo.

Author Desha Peacock travels to San Miguel de Allende, Mexico, each year to facilitate her Sweet Spo
Style LUX Retreats. With the help of her laptop and iPhone, working from abroad has never been easie

the gypsetter

Where to Create When You're Globetrotting

I just love the word GYPSETTER. It's a combo of gypsy and jetsetter. I have a gypsy soul for sure. I grew up in a small town outside of Little Rock, Arkansas, and we didn't travel much when I was a kid. I remember turning to my mother at age twelve and asking, "Why did I have to be born here?"

I just couldn't wait to leave. I made it my mission to travel internationally, which meant that I was the girl traveling across Europe and later Central America, hopping trains and buses, staying in hostels, and living off baguettes and street tacos.

It was brilliant at the time. I learned so much and gained a ton of confidence, but the days of traveling on the cheap for me are *over*. I still want to go, but I want to stay in beautiful places, eat at gorgeous restaurants, and partake in all the activities that I want to without my wallet dictating my decisions.

That's the way of the Gypsetter—traveling in style, a little boho, and very much with an attitude of creativity and freedom.

Some Gypsetters are more gypsy than anything else. The world at large is their home. Others, like myself, migrate with the seasons. I live in Vermont most of the year but travel to Mexico for at least a month or two in the winter.

In this section, we'll meet a Gypsetter whose nest is in constant motion, as well as a few whose wanderlust take them away seasonally or whenever the mood strikes.

Here's how to maintain your *creative work space*, when you are neither here nor there.

Robyn McClendon

I am: Artist, Designer, Authenticity Coach, Gypsetter
My home: Phoenix, Arizona
My style: Bohemian. Eclectic. *A RareBird.*

I love to encourage and inspire others to live a life worth living.

Robyn McClendon is an artist, mixed media painter, papermaker, and bookbinder. She's also an authenticity coach. She studied papermaking and bookbinding as an apprentice, as these art forms were dying in the '80s and only being revived by artists. She's taught at universities and museum systems as an adjunct professor and set up programs in art departments across the nation focusing on the discipline of *books as art.*

Her design experience has won her notable commissions, including creating a distinctive award for Dr. Dorothy Irene Height's Uncommon Height project, which celebrates outstanding contributions to this country's advancement. Previous recipients include Oprah Winfrey, Dr. Maya Angelou, Vanessa Williams, and Vernon Jordan, to name a few. Additionally, she's designed for Essence Communications, Ikea, Target, and UNICEF. Her exhibits have been shown in the Smithsonian Museums and the Corcoran Gallery of Art, and her art can be seen in the permanent collections of the University of Maryland, the National Museum of Women in the Arts, and the Museum of Modern Art.

She also loves to travel.

Travel is very important to me! Wanderlust is in my soul. I'm highly inspired by the sights, sounds, colors, textures, foods, smells, and the way in which various climates/weather affect the landscape and the hardscapes.

Walls weather differently, feathers, stones, and all sorts of found items are completely different as you move around the globe. When I'm in one spot too long, I get very restless. I have to find something to do, some new adventure, even if it's only getting in my car and setting out to the next town or nearby nature spot, or simply a Saturday flea market allows me to travel the world, because you never know what you'll find there.

I have a tendency to move a lot. I've lived in eleven different homes while raising my kids. I homeschooled them, so we could travel and I could give them the gift of experiencing different environments and people in order to broaden their perceptions of the world.

Every year my kids and I go somewhere; last year we spent a month in San Miguel de Allende, a hilltop village in Mexico that had been on my radar for several years. It's a place that I will always go back to. Some places you visit are great to experience, but you're ready to move on and not necessarily return, but not San Miguel.

Working from various home offices/studios as you do, how do you stay organized and on task?

I love travel cases or pouches to keep things organized. I believe in using the latest technology in order to be efficient. Making design deadlines, working with clients, and maintaining online portfolios of my work, it's important to be able to get on the Internet. Also, I'm a big thrifter and treasure hunter. One part of the thrill of making a new spot feel like my own, if only temporarily, is to hit the local flea markets and antique hunts.

I find textiles to cover beds, desk chairs to hang on the walls, baskets for my art supplies, small vases for flowers, and more. I often leave some of my things for the next visitor, but not my textiles or small brass vases—they stay with me!

How does your creative work space(s) help you do the work you were meant to do, especially related to being the fabulous gypsetter that you are?

I'm a big collector, it's something about bringing things from around the world home with me. I'm big on textual material in my art. Archeology runs through my veins; the idea of finding things that are lost and discovering their uses or the stories they have to tell gives me joy.

I love reusing these objects in a new context in my artwork or in my living environment, which in many ways are one and the same. My studio is filled with bits and bobs of all sorts of things found at flea markets or feathers and stones gathered on nature walks.

My mind is stimulated to produce work with soul. Creating in this way reminds me of previous journeys, colors, and textures that speak to me.

Your Creative Work

Besides being an artist, I also love to mentor people to encourage them to go bravely into the world and pursue careers as artists. I help people live their lives the way they really want to live and not settle until some future date. I have ultimately helped many professionals in what I instinctively call authenticity coaching.

Pretty + Practical

I'm really not the best with paperwork, so I keep it pretty basic with a few file drawers. As for my artwork, I use flat files and large metal shelving that allows me to lay the work flat, which is important with artwork. Most of my ephemera, old books, and found objects that I use in my art are stored in a wicker suitcase.

Core Values

My studio is eclectic, loaded with all sorts of inspiration. When I walk into my studio, I like it to look like a *cabinet of curiosities*. I love going to antique stores, especially

the dirty, dusty kind, where some items haven't been touched in months or years. There is a thrill of discovery, like finding something to treasure and to inspire myself. My artwork is the same. My hope is that it inspires others as it inspires me.

Sweet Spot Style Tip

Create the way you like to live. It can be a clean and serene environment or in a gypsy's caravan! I believe it's important to surround ourselves with the things that make us happy. Don't cut corners. Be at your happiest while you create. You can start off in any size space, but make what you really need and want a priority. If for now you only have the corner of the living room, great. But if you desire a large, quiet studio in the sanctuary of your backyard, then make a vision board around this and prioritize until you have it. Oftentimes we can talk ourselves into believing that where we create isn't that important, but it is. It's our lifeblood.

Sometimes I find people will move into a home, and because the builder thought that they should have a dining room, they set that space up in that fashion and never really think about the fact that they could eat in the kitchen and be quite happy. They could use that fantastic dining space for an incredible creative work space. Sometimes just giving ourselves the permission to live a little unconventionally in order to have a *life worth living* is really all we need to do.

Best Advice

Just begin doing what makes you happy. Don't compare yourself to others. Instead, channel that desire into inspiration so you can create your own perfect place.

I find that the details are in the doing! Just begin.

Find Robyn online at robynmcclendon.com
and on Instagram @rarebirds.

Vienda Maria

I am: Writer, Mentor, Creative
My home: Global Citizen
My style: Minimalist. Bohemian. Artistic.

Freedom is something that you cultivate from within.

I met Vienda online in a popular virtual business school. I was attracted to her free-flow Gypset life*style*, half gypsy, half jetsetter. We've been online biz buddies for several years now, and I am always intrigued and fascinated by how she skips across the globe, laptop and coconut chai latte in hand. Vienda has become an expert at designing and living a life that truly reflects her desires and purpose.

Vienda, tell us about your business and how you've created this amazing career/life*style* for yourself?
Unlike most people, I didn't have to jump the fence from a corporate lifestyle to a freedom-fueled one. Straight out of university, I had these beautiful opportunities to travel the world working at international music festivals as a contracted event organizer and artist manager. I did it for almost five years, which gave me plenty of time to really dig into discovering myself and what is truly important to me, while fulfilling my dreams of traveling the world and having lots of fun.

By the time that I had enough of music festival life, I knew there was no way I could work for someone else in a corporate environment, and so my search began, with lifestyle being the anchor for it. I didn't really care about

what I did, as long as I was living a life that offered me the lifestyle that I wanted, which included plenty of creative expression, freedom, and travel.

I started blogging about travel, spirituality, life, and psychology—a passion of mine after studying it for years—and one day a woman emailed me and asked me to coach her through some life challenges she was experiencing. My writing and mentoring business slowly grew from that point and now is a thriving enterprise that supports me and gives back to the world in ways beyond my dreams.

Staying Organized

Traveling with a business means that I have had to become very disciplined and efficient! I work literally anywhere I can: airports, cafés, and hotel rooms being my main work spaces. I generally work about four to five hours per day and organize my tasks into blocks. For example, answering emails first thing every morning, mentoring clients and Skype meetings happen on Tuesday and Saturday, writing tasks are done on Wednesday and Thursday, Friday is

dedicated to PR and building relationships, social media I spend up to an hour on most days, and I try to have Sunday and Monday off as much as possible.

Traveling requires a certain amount of flexibility, however, so even though I have a structure to stay on top of things, I also tend to live quite intuitively and let things go in their own way, which means some days I might work eight hours straight and others not at all.

Rituals

I think it's really important to know your own natural cycles and rhythms and to work with those. I always feel most inspired and eager to get things done in the morning, so I harness that time and ensure that I make the best use of it so I have the rest of the day to simply enjoy life.

I also notice that I have less energy around the new moon and more energy around the full moon, so I adjust my calendar with more or fewer tasks accordingly. We can't expect ourselves to go full steam ahead 100 percent of the time; women are simply not made that way, and when we honor our own natural rhythms and work with them, the results speak for themselves.

Beyond that, my rituals are very simple. Traveling so much requires me to use my own body as an anchor to stay grounded no matter where I find myself, so getting plenty of sleep, eating fresh produce, moving my body, drinking enough water, and spending time in nature are paramount to staying in the zone and getting my work done. As long as I put my self-care first, I'm good!

Freedom

As a writer and mentor, I get to determine my working hours, how I grow and manage my business, when to push, and when to pull back. All of these elements provide me with unlimited independence and freedom to live in the way that feels most aligned, purposeful, and truthful for me.

Freedom being one of my highest values, I get to cultivate that feeling as an experience in my lifestyle and in my work, which truly is a dream. I can't imagine there being a better way than entrepreneurship to facilitate the lifestyle that I have and love.

Biggest Challenge

Unreliable Internet has got to be the number one challenge of working internationally and on the road! Even right now, as I am writing these words in the restaurant of our hotel in Thailand, the connection is coming in and out, and I just have to be patient and roll with it. As much as I can be organized and plan ahead to ensure that I'm connected and online when I need to be, especially on those days that I have client calls, there are no guarantees. I've just learned to be very fluid with those challenges and work around them.

I'm a huge believer in divine timing and that whatever is meant to be will be, so instead of stressing and worrying about it, I do my best, I show up, and do my work every day, and when things don't work out, I believe that there

is a higher purpose to it and let it go. Traveling teaches you that life isn't something you can control, so you might as well just enjoy the ride and make the most of it!

The Nest

After twelve years of traveling the world, I have absolutely come to a place where I am craving to nest, and I couldn't be more excited about it! One of the biggest lessons I have learned over the years is that freedom is something that you cultivate within, and while I will always be a free spirit, I am looking forward to bringing that into a more grounded space. My partner and I are headed to the West Coast of Canada, where he grew up, with plans to buy a cute little old house, renovate it, and turn it into a home base for us.

I have cajoled him into promising to build me an office space in the attic with a round porthole window. And, I cannot wait to decorate our house with all the treasures I have collected and put into storage from all around the world! It's going to be an interesting feat: bringing all of the pieces I've collected from various corners of the globe into one space. Settling down for me simply means creating a more permanent home space from which I can work and travel, something I haven't had for a really, really long time.

Sweet Spot Style Living

I absolutely love the term sweet spot, and for me it's really about living from my intuition. When I am at the leading edge of my creativity, my self-expression and my message, I feel unstoppable. It truly is a sweet spot! I think it's really about living out your highest self in terms of what you want for yourself and your life, at the crossover of what your gifts are and what you can give. Living in your sweet spot is pure magic!

Dream Job As A Kid

There is no simple answer to that. My very first memory of wanting to be something was a mermaid. I trained hard every day for about a year in our neighbor's pool, holding my breath and swimming like a mermaid, so that one day I would have the skills necessary for mermaiding. Those dreams were eventually crushed by some pragmatic adult, and so the jobs I envisioned for myself following were: nun, actress, lawyer, and psychologist. Never had I imagined that I would end up making a living from my writing. I always saw writing as something I did privately, away from the eyes of the public, to soothe my soul.

Tips To Create A Laptop Lifestyle

Drop your plan B and commit to yourself and your dreams. So many people say they want to live this kind of lifestyle, but they find endless excuses why they can't. And while those reasons are practical and logical enough, the truth is that they are rooted in fear. Fear that it won't work out, fear that they will run out of money, fear of being ridiculed.

I like to see fear as the doorway to untapped potential, so I always like to lean into my fears and see where they take me, which is always far more fulfilling and exciting than playing it safe in the arena that we already know. That thing that you dream of and are afraid of—do it and don't look back.

Best Advice

It sounds so cliché, but if you want to do great things in the world, you have to be unapologetically you. When you share that love and inspiration you have for whatever it is that turns you on with the world, great things start to happen. There are no magic formulas or systems that will help you *get it right*. When you share that passion and fire for whatever it is you love to do in the world, you become magnetic.

Find Vienda online at ViendaMaria.com, on Instagram @viendam, and on Facebook at Vienda Maria.

Bianca Gignac

I am: Boss Lady, Traveler, Rule Breaker, Mother
My home: La Spezia, Italy, and Vancouver Island, Canada
My style: Feminine. Eclectic. Natural.

Do it yesterday. Don't underestimate what you're capable of or stand in your own way.

I met Bianca in Italy at one of the workshops her company, Italian Fix, hosted with Justina Blakeney. At the workshop, I not only learned a lot about social media and branding from Justina, I also made some great connections and friends— some of whom are in this book! Bianca has continued to be a support in my business and life, so I'm super excited to share her story as a model for success. If you have dreams of an international laptop lifestyle, read on.

Your Creative Work

I own a travel media company and help people travel more. Each year we offer travel experiences to the prettiest places in Italy via italianfix.com. We also help DIYers travel with our travel guides at gigiguides.com.

I arrived at this journey in a very roundabout way! I was broke and going to art college and was awarded a study scholarship to a summer program in Italy. Since my crappy studio apartment had a lovely view of a parking lot and a garbage dumpster, I jumped at the opportunity to study in Italy for the summer. In Italy, I ended up meeting an amazing person who's now my husband.

After I graduated with my BFA in my midtwenties, I moved to Italy for a few years, got married there, and started my company in 2011 after my daughter was born. We don't live full time in Italy anymore, but instead split our time between two places.

I built the company from the ground up, with zero money, as a side job while I was working and mothering. I went full time a few years into the business, once I doubled my revenue. That was the tipping point and inspired me to commit big.

I knew in my gut it was the right move for me because my company is really built around my strengths and interests and something that I would do for free: share cool finds with others, share my knowledge of Italy, and share a worldview that travel and experiences are more valuable than "stuff" will ever be.

I feel so fortunate that I get to do work that's creative and lights me up, and that I get to work with some of my favorite people in the world—my team and customers.

Staying Organized

I could move anywhere tomorrow and still run the company. I have a laptop, and all my work tech fits into one petite carry-on.

I work at home, in hotels, cafés, on boats, or in planes. I work anywhere and everywhere.

I manage a virtual team spread out over a few different time zones, and we collaborate inside the same tech. The secret is to work with your team via SaaS-based solutions, which is a fancy way of saying we use software that lives in the cloud. Even if my laptop fell into the ocean tomorrow, I would still be able to work from my phone. If being mobile and working from anywhere appeals to you, my advice is to build your company using the cloud from day one.

We use Dropbox to store large data, a whole lotta Google Drive to hold files and collaborate, plus software like Basecamp, Asana, and Trello to manage projects and editorial calendars. Oh, and I'm pretty addicted to Slack, our team chat.

When you want to automate sales processes, create marketing funnels, or store sensitive customer information, you can buy more robust CRM (customer relationship management) software, like Salesforce, Ontraport, Infusionsoft, etc. With a small combination of these tools, you can create, manage, and oversee your business with just an Internet connection. It's by nature pretty organized and efficient. I love talking about this stuff, and I love the era we're in. It feels boundless.

How do you create a virtual work space that facilitates creativity for yourself and others?

Creativity is essential to building exceptional products and environments that our customers love, and that will hopefully leave a legacy in the industry we're in. But I find that most creatives need constraints or we don't get anything done! Because I have endless ideas for projects and products that I'm stoked to release into the market, I try to focus strategically on the bandwidth of what I or my team can create and deliver within the constraints of time and resources.

It may seem counterintuitive to work that way for some of us artsy types, but I swear it's been the one thing that has helped me get traction and carry my enthusiasm to the finish line. Once we define the constraints (like time or budget or features), we have a starting place from which to start dreaming about what can be built.

You have a beautiful little girl; how do you manage all you do and be a momma?

I'm really proud of being a working mother, and I feel like passing on the values of self-sufficiency is something insanely vital to the generation of kids we're raising. My sweet daughter, Flora, is eight, and she's seen my husband and me work hard but also make family time a priority. That's probably the Italian side of my life talking: don't take the day-to-day so seriously! I love to model to my kiddo that life is created intentionally from a series of choices. The greatest gift I feel like I could transfer is a deep sense of self-worth and self-reliance, and so I try and show those traits just by being myself.

Working at home and weaving it all together just feels true to who I am. It's not a perfect science, it's an evolving art. Becoming a mom was the biggest catalyst for me realizing that being the queen bee of my own schedule was mandatory for creating the lifestyle I wanted.

How does your current biz model help facilitate your ideal lifestyle?

Instead of business models, I like to think of life models, because that's the simplest way for me to think of what I'm trying to build that brings together work and life. My company business model is both service based and information based, and before I add any new projects, I just try to lean on my intuition and stay true to my vision of how I want to live, how I want to raise my daughter, and how to give my marriage the attention it needs to thrive.

That's how I filter which business move to make next. I also lean on advisors who've been there before with things related to finance, hiring, and product-market fit, so I can move forward with less friction.

Biggest Challenge

Growing a company is just challenging, whether I stay in one place or move around. It's still just showing up every day to "you" and having the capacity to deal with the challenges at hand. There are definitely days when I just feel like going back to bed with a bag of cookies, but other days I feel unstoppable. As time goes on in business, I feel the latter more often because I've flexed the *I-can-do-this* mentality for more time.

I really face all challenges with an attitude of personal growth, and I'm a constant student of life. I'm a voracious reader and that fuels my appetite for growth, as docs meeting our customers personally and other entrepreneurs around the world at events I host or attend.

Sweet Spot Style Living

My belief is that the world holds beauty and opportunity for us all if we're patient enough with ourselves to discover how that can unfold. That *knowing* is the sweet spot for me.

If you're reading this and feel like you're not currently working in your genius zone, then ask yourself these questions:

What do I enjoy doing in my free time?

What would I do even if I wasn't paid for it?

What would I choose to do if I could never retire?

What do people ask me for advice about?

How am I useful?

I think asking hard questions is the start, and the middle is having faith in yourself that you'll eventually come up with the answers. Not being too afraid to try is the biggest step you can make to move yourself closer to the person you want to be. But sitting around thinking about it won't do anything—you gotta take action to make it happen!

Dream Job As A Kid

I grew up on an island in Canada, which was a laid-back place where people worked to live, not lived to work. Growing up in that scene meant I didn't have grand career ambitions as a kid, and I was rarely ever asked [what I wanted to do]! I've always been intensely creative and entrepreneurial from a really young age. When I wasn't scaling cedar limbs to build tree forts, up to my gum boots in pond water building rafts, or riding my horse with friends, I was scheming up innovative ways to help neighbors and family members part with their pocket change.

My earliest preteen forays into business were gardening, dog walking, choreographing dance routines, and writing a magazine about Madonna. My first *real job* was at age eleven, and I've been working ever since. Making my own money has always symbolized choice and freedom, and those values are still massively important to me today.

Tips For Leading The Laptop Lifestyle

Do it yesterday. Don't underestimate what you're capable of or stand in your own way.

Find Bianca at italianfix.com
or on Instagram @italianfix and @gigiguides.

Caroline White

I am: Photographer/Videographer
My home: Echo Park Neighborhood of Los Angeles
Space: WeWork Pasadena

Your Creative Work

I'm a lifestyle and personal branding portrait photographer and videographer. I travel a ton—most often to New York City, Chicago, London, Paris, and other parts of Europe. I also do humanitarian causes—I've filmed at special needs schools in India and elephant sanctuaries in Thailand. I teach workshops on photography and small business building. I lead women's photography retreats to Cuba. And I have an online print shop. So, yeah, a lot of balls in the air!

Your Creative Work Space

I was drawn to WeWork's super cute digs and decor, and then realized their WiFi is 100 times faster than my WiFi at home, so that comes in super handy when uploading high-resolution photos and videos, as well as the all-important cloud storage that keeps my work safe and also accessible while I travel.

I actually like the short drive to WeWork, when I can prepare my mind to get productive and focused on editing and organizing photos and video files. They have free coffee, tea, and beer (on tap!), plus lots of other perks and community events, and there's WeWork offices all over the world.

When I get home, I can mostly let go of certain work tasks. I find that compartmentalization very helpful.

Caroline can be found online at
carolinewhitephotography.com and on IG @carolinewphoto.

the tiny space

How To Design a Creative Work Space in a Closet, Nook, or Cranny

The freedom-based life*style* is taking over the old nine-to-five model. These days, lots of folks are trading in the McMansion for a tiny house. Whether to save money or to make less of an impact on the environment, one thing is for sure, *small* is in.

Yet, just because you have a small space, that doesn't mean you have to give up your creative work space. In this chapter we'll see how folks are getting creative with their small and tiny spaces by creating offices out of some pretty unusual places.

The Family Control Center, designed by John Donkin

This space, located in a new urban home, was designed by architect John Donkin for a young family-to-be. The desk is located in a small alcove in the dining room (the hub of the house) and contains all that is needed to manage a busy family.

The space is simple, with suspended shelves, a few drawers, and space for a laptop. The chalk on the wall is an ever-changing ornament, reflecting the rhythm of their lives.

Tips for Designing a Family Control Center

1. **Pick a central area** of your home where you have easy access.

2. **Design the space for your specific needs.** Do you need storage for papers, art, journals, or other office supplies?

3. **Measure the height of the desk** to your favorite chair to make sure you have the right fit.

4. **Leave space from the desk to the wall** to allow for discrete wire management; one inch should do it.

5. **Add chalk paint** so little creative bosses can help manage the household.

John can be found online at jdarchitect.ca.

Anna Margaret

I am: Proprietress of Le Souk, Le Souk
My home: Portland, Oregon
My style: Eclectic. Boho. Luxe.

Surround yourself with positivity and beauty and you will exude positivity beautifully!

Your Creative Work

I opened my first brick and mortar shop in 2010, with a focus on globally sourced home goods, small, independent clothing lines, and locally handcrafted children's items. Five years in, I realized that my babies were no longer babies, and I was starting to have time to refocus on my own interests again. So I rebranded my business, dropped the children's section, moved locations, and opened up Le Souk Le Souk, a boutique inspired by textiles, travel, and female strength—all of my clothing designers are women! As retail trends continued to shift, I decided at the beginning of 2017 to take my shop exclusively online so that I could worry less about overhead and focus more on my family and creative self.

How does your current creative work space help you do the work you were meant to do?

I am a very visual person; I know exactly what I want every corner of my home to look like before I start decorating. I knew that I needed light, greenery, and art to feel inspired while working on my website, filling orders, and communicating with customers. My work space makes me feel happy and motivated to share beautiful treasures with my customers.

Staying Organized

Well, I don't always stay on task. I frequently get distracted with watering plants, toasting a bagel, or Instagram. However, I do keep three calendars: one small organizer in my purse for *everything*, one large calendar in my office for daily work tasks, and one on my phone for my kids' schedules. Plus [I use] baskets and drawers. If everything has its own place, then it's easy to clean up throughout the day. Clutter drives me crazy!

Biggest Challenge

Lighting has been difficult. My office was originally a small closet without an interior light. Plus, we live in an A-frame home, so the slanted side walls don't have any exterior windows. Thankfully, my dad has basic electrician skills, so he has been a huge help.

Pretty + Practical

I only keep what I need on a daily basis in my office. All of my shop inventory is organized in the garage, as are my shipping supplies. I make an effort to put everything back into drawers, files, and baskets after I finish working each afternoon.

Sweet Spot Style Living

Living in my sweet spot means that I get to appreciate my home, family, and backyard every day!

Core Values

I believe that what and who we surround ourselves with become a part of us, so surround yourself with positivity and beauty and you will exude positivity beautifully!

Style Tips

A lovely work space doesn't have to cost a lot, although I'm super lucky to have a talented artist as my partner [Srijon Chowdhury], who hand-painted my botanical walls. There are many cost-effective ways to create the look of wallpaper now with paint, vinyl, etc. I sourced my baskets, drawers, and chair at Homegoods and Ikea. My desk is simply high-grade plywood from Home Depot.

You can find Anna online at lesouklesouk.com
and on Instagram @lesouklesouk.

For tots and teens

Creating A Work + Play Sweet Spot Space

By now, you probably see the importance of having your own creative work space. If you have children and want to keep your creative work space intact, I highly recommend that you help them create their own sweet spot space.

When creating a work or play space, be sure to leave some "white space." This open space allows for movement, as well as a portal for ideas.

Amy Kavelaris (Amy Kavs)

I am: Fine Artist, Author, Illustrator
My home: The Midwest
My style: Imaginative. Eclectic. Feminine.
Handcrafted.

Sometimes I fail miserably at balancing family, friends, and work, but my prayer is to do this to the best of my ability. That is when I'm in my sweet spot.

Amy Kavelaris owns a fine art school for children and adults, sells her custom art worldwide on Instagram, and is an author and children's book illustrator. She's a wife, mom, teacher, and a fine artist. As she says, *this is my favorite gig yet!*

As an artist and mother, how do you balance the two?
Naturally, I wouldn't say I'm a strict schedule person, but I've found that as a business owner who now works mostly from home with a toddler and babe on the way, a schedule has become essential for me. But flexibility is key. It's no secret that when my home is clean, I'm probably in between projects. When I am knee-deep in deadlines, my house is a disaster. Although it makes me itch, I have learned that it is okay. Like my mother always says, "As a woman you can do everything you want . . . just not always at the same time." Typically, I get most done during [my daughter's] naps and late at night. I know these moments are fleeting while our daughter is not in school, so I am trying to cherish my time with her. Walks and mini adventures are always built into our days. I also love that my daughter gets to join me as I work and learn that we all have responsibilities.

This is a fun question because our Mila is insanely (perhaps even unusually) happy creating right along next to me. When I was in the process of writing my first book, even just at fifteen months, she would grab a pillow, lay it on the floor at my feet, and draw endlessly on paper. As she gets older, we have to change up our routine. What started as wearing Mila in her carrier while I painted now involves dancing to Pandora's "Hipster Cocktail Party," Mindy Gledhill, and Louis Armstrong, and lots of snacks!

I usually let her gesso my canvases. I'm so in love with having her fingerprints all over my work as well. It makes me breathless to watch one of our greatest tiny masterpieces enjoy doing what I believe our Ultimate Artist created us to do . . . embrace the joy of creating.

I would adore her whether she was into my work or not, but it has been especially joyful having my daughter creating by my side. She also loves to travel. Lately, I have traveled more than usual for work, and it's fun to have Mila in tow when possible.

Biggest Challenge

There are certainly roadblocks. Work/life balance issues. Finding time! Self-doubt. I am constantly a work in progress with these. But in all honesty, after having a myriad of career moves that just were not hitting my sweet spot, I

cherish every day the opportunity to work in a field in which I come alive. My husband is a huge support. I am simply grateful to do what I love.

Sweet Spot Style Living

Finding my sweet spot since becoming a mom has meant letting go of control of my own life, and I have found so much freedom in that. Believing in my craft, embracing imperfection, and finding a balance is always a process.

Finding time to unplug from an Internet-based business and making time to connect can be difficult, but freeing and essential. I am most successful when my family is happy and I can find balance in my work.

Mommy Guilt

I've come to the realization that guilt often needs to be reevaluated for the level of its truth. For me anyway. I often find myself overthinking and second-guessing how much time I put into certain projects or lesson planning. On

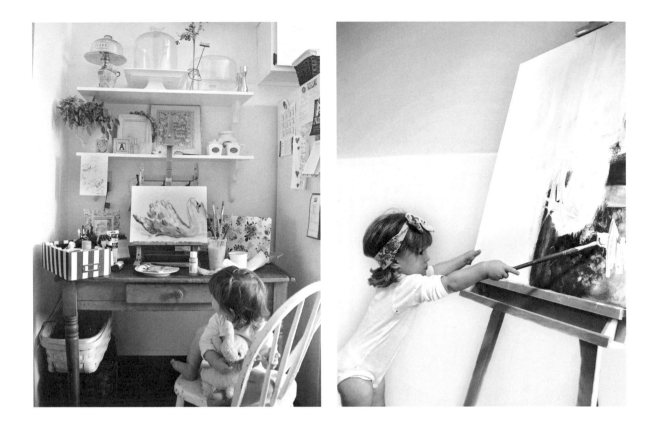

the other hand, I think it's valuable for our daughter to watch and learn the discipline that comes along with running your own business, having a strong work ethic, and staying true to your word. It takes consistent checking in with myself to evaluate what is truth, what is not, making sure I am taking on enough, but not what I've come to know as too much for me.

What's one thing you hope your daughter learns from you?
"Whatever your hand finds to do, do it with all your heart," Colossians 3:23. Use your abilities to bring joy to others, not to glorify yourself. Work hard. And constantly surround yourself with the very best content and influences to grow in whatever you were created to do.

Any other tips on how to maintain your own creative work space and do what you are meant to do while also being a great mom?
If being a *great mom* means you love with all you have, try your very best, but don't have all the answers, I suppose I can answer this question!

First, keep your creative space saturated with a lot of natural light if possible! Also, surround yourself with what you love; for me, that's family heirlooms, nature, or fresh blooms. Your creative soul will breathe its deepest when it is echoing to the core of who you are.

Interweaving passion and daily tasks is completely inspiring to me. For example, my creative work space has recently been majorly downsized with our move to the city, so I will have an easel in the kitchen next to my desk and my meal planning. Time is slotted for each. It's not chaotic, but I always try to live as a part of my art and around those that inspire. If I am working on paintings, they hang on my walls so that I can live with them until I am happy with their completion. On the other hand, if I am cooking or cleaning, I spend that time in prayer, with music on that inspires me, or I'm listening to one of my favorite speakers streaming online. Life's too short not to enjoy the little things.

My best advice to stay fresh and creative: strive to incorporate being a creative into your life by giving back. The gifts we make for others; the creative ways we give in our community. And cheering on others in their own creative processes, whatever they may be . . . *that* is what gives me life!

Find Amy online at bloomprintstudio.com
and on Instagram @amykavs.

Sara Banner

I am: Fiber Artist
My home: New Cumberland, Pennsylvania
My style: Modern. Eclectic. Simplicity.

It's really important that my work space and my children's [space] feel very personal.

Her Creative Work Space

My daughter's little desk was a local antique store find. I only paid about $20 for the desk and chair. It was perfect for this little corner in her room. She loves to use the space to play with her dollhouse, color, and read. As with all of our spaces, we try to keep things fun and bohemian but also clutter-free.

The basket helps to contain her favorite books, and I'm a big fan of the little Target dollar-bin buckets that hold crayons and markers. To make them easier to set out, I put them into an old wooden box that I picked up from a flea market for $3.

We rotate our wall decor quite a bit, but I'm loving her little paintings simply taped to the wall with washi tape. We also recently added a little shelf—made out of some of my macramé cord and a piece of barnwood from her grandparent's farm—to this corner. Finally, you can always find a plant or two in every space in our home. My kids even name them!

Staying Organized

Both of my children are really great about cleaning up after themselves. We've made it a priority as a family, so I always try to give them baskets and bins to make cleanup and organization as painless as possible. For me, when every item has its place, it's easier to stay organized.

Children's Creative Work Space Tips

It's really important that my work space and my children's feel very personal. I love looking at the portrait hanging above my desk and thinking of my grandmother and my mother. It may be a small thing, but the shelf in my daughter's room reminds us of trips to her grandparent's farm. I want our home to feel like us.

Find Sara online at theforestfern.com
and on Instagram @the_forestfern.

Marian Bouma

I am: Advising Nurse, Creative Soul
My home: Leusden, Netherlands
My style: Eclectic Mix of Retro-Vintage. Modern. A Touch of Urban Jungle.

My job title is advising nurse at the medical department of a health insurance company. My creative pursuits include interior styling, refurbishing furniture I find at thrift stores, creating things from old stuff; for example, sewing pillows from old army bags and making baskets from old bicycle tires . . . anything where I can be creative.

His Creative Work Space

My son is the youngest of the three. He found that his brother's and sister's rooms were always more cozy and interesting. He yearned for a *big boy's room*. The green palette is a cool, yet cozy color and works well with his love of dinosaurs. The mix of vintage and new furniture makes it an original room that none of his friends have!

Biggest Challenges

There were two big challenges when it came to designing my son's room. One was the toys: there are so many! We solved that problem by storing them in some black Ikea boxes neatly in his closet. The other challenge was that I didn't want a standard, ordinary room full of brand-new furniture from a box store. Instead, I mixed some things from Ikea and the rest from thrift stores, secondhand shops, and things I found online.

Sweet Spot Style

Living in my sweet spot means a warm, stylish, and colorful place.

Mommy Guilt

I work twenty hours a week at an insurance company. Now my kids are a little older—eight, twelve, and fourteen years—so they are a bit more independent. This gives me more time for my creative pursuits. Sometimes I wish I had more time to be creative, but I know as my kids get older, I'll have more *me time*. I actually don't have mommy guilt, I'm just exhausted at the end of the day . . . ha, ha!

Be original! My son is very creative on his own. He doesn't need other kids to think of something original. I treasure that!

You can find Marian on Instagram at @fijninhuis.

Desha Peacock

I am: LifeSTYLE / Small Biz Coach + Founder of Sweet Spot Style + Author
My home: Brattleboro, Vermont
My style: Cozy. Eclectic. Personal.

Everyone needs their own sweet spot space, but there's no need to spend a fortune. Shop your house first.

Where My Daughter Creates

My daughter and I both have several places in our home where we write, dream, and create. These places morph as our interests change. Right now, my daughter has two primary play/workstations. Lately, I've noticed that she takes her decorating cues from me. After I moved my office into my bedroom, she became interested in a similar setup.

Shop the House

Creating my daughter's bedroom office took less than one day. We looked around the house and found her desk, which was previously a sideboard in our foyer. We painted it white and placed it under some existing shelves. We grabbed a chair off the patio, added one of her pretty gold-and-white pillows from the bed, and, presto, she had a new creative work space.

The Cabin

We have this little room between our back porch and garage that we call *the cabin.* If you have my first book,

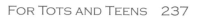

Create the Style You Crave on a Budget You Can Afford, you'll see that my daughter and I renovated it together. It's gone through several iterations but currently acts as a quiet space for my daughter to dream, relax, and play with her friends.

The desk and chair were found for free at our town dump and recycling center. The dollhouse was discovered at our local thrift shop. The large wooden trunk came from my husband's father. The horse painting was a gift from a stranger at

a wonderful summer tag sale. We picked up the rug in Tunisia, purchased over hot tea, as is the custom. Hanging from the ceiling are yards and yards of finger weavings that my daughter made.

Sweet Spot Style Tips for Creating Kid's Spaces

1. No matter your square footage, kids need their own creative work space, even if it's just a tiny nook.

2. Create the space with your child. Ask them what they want to do in the space and let that inform the design. Do they need a place to draw or write, or would they prefer a place to lounge and read?

3. Be patient knowing children's tastes often change quickly. If your little girl wants bright pink walls (and that will make you nauseous), compromise with bright accents such as throw pillows or other accessories.

4. Celebrate your child's creativity by showcasing their most prized handmade treasures.

5. Start young. Allow them to make a big mess. Creativity is messy, but also teach them how to respect their space by cleaning up after they're done creating for the day.

6. The best way to keep a tidy space is to minimize stuff. Our rule is: one thing in means one thing out.

7. Small space? No problem. Small kids love hidden spots. Can you create a nook under the stairs or in a closet? Big kids love privacy. Could you create something amazing in the attic, basement, shed, or garage?

Final thoughts

In this book, we've talked about the importance of creative expression and how your physical space can enhance, or help bring forth, this energy. You've heard the stories of interior stylists, photographers, bloggers, graphic designers, authors, online shopkeepers, and artists. Each one sharing their unique perspective on how to create a sweet spot work space.

I hope you can take these stories and images to heart. Let them inspire you to tap into your own beautiful essence so that you too can create your own magical creative work space.

Let me know how it goes!

xo Desha Peacock

acknowledgments

Huge gratitude to all the contributors who took the time to answer intimate questions about their creative lives and share their beautiful spaces. Without you, this book would not have been possible.

To friends Nicole Liloia, Stasia Savasuk, and Cara Paige, who have given me their friendship, eyes, and hands to help this book come along.

To Suzanne Kingsbury, who said "Your book is the gateway to your career." You were right. Thank you.

Thank you to Skyhorse Publishing, particularly Abigail Gehring, who helped me stay focused on my sweet spot when she suggested I write this book. Thanks to my editor, Brooke Rockwell, for your patience, insight, and keen eye.

To all the photographers, particularly Leslie Woodward, who traveled all the way to Mexico for some of the shots in this book and helped me create and style the cover. You are such a generous soul. To Jo Chattman, who styled and shot many of the photos of my home. Your talents are many.

To Candle in the Night for lending me their beautiful rugs. To my dear assistant, Sarah Bennett, who managed all the book communication and assisted in every part of its design and production. You are a true gem!

To my daughter, Iyla, who is so generous in her love and support of her multi-passionate mom. I adore you with all my heart. And to my husband, Matt, for helping out so I could take the time to pull this together. Finally, heartfelt gratitude for my mother, who reads every word I write and continues to remind me to just be myself. That's the best advice a daughter can receive. Thanks, mom.

photo credits

p. iii, vi–viii, xvii, xix, xxii, 4, 64–77, p. 220, 238 Jo Chattman

p. iv, 22–29 Anisa Rrapaj

p. x–xv, 102–108 Emil Larsson

p. xxi, xxvi, 150–155 Sarah Bennett

p. xxiv, 48–55 Justina Blakeney

p. xxvii Kyle Born Photography

p. 6–3 Anna Louise Harris

p. 14, 16–21 Holly Becker

p. 15 Anouschka Rokebrand

p. 30--35 Casey Brodley

p. 36–40 Tessa Neustadt

p. 42–47 Casamidy

p. 56–63 Jen Smith of Honey Lake Studio

p. 78, 122–125 Ekaterina Ivankina

p. 80–84 Yolanda Ataraxia

p. 86, 89–93 Louise Gale

p. 87 Reine Sloan

p. 94–100 Zipporah Photography

p. 101 Flora Bowley

p. 110–115 Casey Gammon

p. 116–121 Amy McIntyre

p. 126, 184 Leslie Woodward

p. 128–131 Nazanin Pouresmaili

p. 132, 134–135 Frederick Paige, Paige Photo Printz

p. 133 Maya Oren

p. 136–143 Evi Abeler

p. 144, 146–147, 149 Liz Kamarul

p. 145 Ty Milford

p. 148 Tim Kamarul

p. 156, 228, 230–231 Sara Banner

p. 157, 229 Juliana Bird Photography

p. 160–162,165, 167 Marcella Kovac, styled by Madeline Rhodes of Oh My Gemini.

p. 163–164, 166, 168, 170–171, 172, second from top, Victoria Gloria Photography, styled by Madeline Rhodes of Oh My Gemini

p. 169 Jen Brister of Story & Gold

p. 172, top and bottom, 173 by Anaise Prince Photography

p. 174, 176–177, 202, 206–208, 240, 251 Caroline White Photography

p. 175 Brittany Ambridge

p. 178, 196–199 Luke Marshall

p. 180–183 Dominic Naranjo

p. 186–187, 191–192 Shen Daughtry

p. 188–190 Robyn McClendon

p. 194–195 Vienda Maria

p. 200 Jess Shirley

p. 203–205 Azzurra Biagi

p. 210 Jess Safko

p. 212, 216–219 Mikola Accuardi

p. 214 Justin Van Leeuwen - JVL Photography

p. 222–227 Nick Kavelaris

p. 232, 234–235 Marian Bouma

p. 233 Sarah Bouma

p. 237 Rebecca Wright

resource guide

Some of My Favorite Online Shops

Alexandra Fraser Artist/ Stylist on IG @alexandravstudio

Alex uses a variety of earth pigments and mixed fibers with plaster to create textured art inspired by the topography of the land and the ever changing environment. Her work is featured on the cover of this book. It's the large piece on the table to the left.

DENY Designs—www.denydesigns.com

A modern, think-outside-the-box home furnishings company with a variety of fun household accessories. Customize orginal statement pieces by adding a personal image or selecting artwork from the DENY Artist Galleries.

Experimental Vintage—www.experimentalvintage.com

This is a cozy little working studio and rug showcase in the historical Baker Building in the heart of north Portland, Oregon. Anna, the owner, loves to have people drop by to talk textiles, plants, vintage, and coffee.

FAYCE— www.faycetextiles.com

FAYCE creates hand-screened textiles and printed wallpaper using water-based, nontoxic inks and dyes. Owner and designer Kim Rosen draws all of the patterns by hand and strives to create work that is subtle yet intricate, modern yet classic.

Green Body + Green Home—www.greenbodygreenhome.bigcartel.com

At Green Body + Green Home, you'll find beautiful, ethically sourced rugs, pillows, and leather products for your home office or studio.

Luna Reece—www.lunareece.com

Art and ceramics for the modern world. Planters, pottery, plates, art, and other modern forms that bring a fresh vibe. As seen on the front and back cover.

May Designs—www.maydesigns.com

This lifestyle brand specializes in customized notebooks, stationery, and more. The flagship product is the May Book, a simple notebook that can be customized to reflect your unique style. Available in three sizes, it lays flat and fits nicely in a purse. Oprah and I agree, May Design notebooks and stationery are one of our favorite things!

Melissa Jenkins Art—www.melissamaryjenkinsart.ca

Natural inks and abstract art. Check out her originals and hoop art.

Nudes and Candles—www.nudesandcandles.com/IG @nudes_and_candles

Handmade candles by Jo Chattman. As seen on the cover.

Portland Apron Company—www.portlandaproncompany.com

Using organic and sustainable fabrics, such as linen and hemp, Portland Apron Company creates handmade aprons and pinafores in a small studio in Portland, Oregon. Since the beginning, the company's focus has been the same: simple design, quality fabrics, and durable stitches to support a sustainable and creative life.

The Rise and Fall—www.theriseandfall.com

A small, family-owned design studio based in the hills of western Massachusetts featuring fun, functional, and affordable design. Using local materials, all goods are handmade. I love their banners, napkins, and tea towels. Their canvas plant holder is featured on the cover of this book.

Secret Holiday & Co.—www.secretholidayco.com

Handcrafted affirmation banners by Ashley Brown Durand in Western Massachusetts, as seen on page 64 & 72 in Jo Chattman's studio. Banner quote by Emily Dickinson, as seen on pages 64, 66 & 72.

Society6—www.society6.com

The artwork on Society6 is created by hundreds of thousands of artists from around the world. Find art prints, stretched canvases, techy cases, rugs, tapestries, and much more.

Taylor Ceramics—www.carataylor.com

Taylor Ceramics provides a line of handmade porcelain vessels and planters for the home and table.

My Favorite "Local" Shops Around The World

Northampton, Massachusetts

Sticks and Bricks—www.sticksandbricksshop.com

This design and build shop is located at 9 Market Street in Northampton. A unique combination of workshop and retail space where they make one-of-a-kind furniture from old and reclaimed materials. Owner Liz Karney works right in the store, where you can find finished pieces, bits and bobs to inspire, and a selection of work from other artists. Her services range from making custom furniture to in-home design consultations.

Kestrel Shop—www.kestrelshopt.com

Specializing in handmade products such as jewelry, planters, terrariums, and bath products, as well as home goods from art work to candles, tea towels to ornaments.

Turners Falls, Massachusetts

LOOT—www.loottheshop.com

Located in the downtown area, LOOT offers a unique variety of industrial artifacts and handmade goods. Find: tables, chalkboards, bowties, bowls, fabric, hats, signs, buttons, Elvis sideburns, scrap paper, photographs, and more.

Sayulita, Mexico

Evoke the Spirit—www.evokethespirit.com

One-of-a-kind pieces that will make your home office or studio sparkle. Check out their hand-painted skulls and locally made textiles.

Schoolhouse Electric & Supply Co.—www.schoolhouse.com

In collaboration with talented makers, artists, and crafts people, this shop provides a variety of quality-one-of-a-kind goods with stories of their own. Products range from analog clocks to lighting and furniture.

Magnolia Market at the Silos—www.magnoliamarket.com

Who doesn't love Chip and Joanna Gaines? Shop Magnolia to find all kinds of beautiful home decor items and much, much more.

Altiplano—www.altiplano.com

A small company based in southern Vermont and Lake Atitlan, Guatemala. Working with many cooperative groups, small family businesses, and their own fair trade workshop, Altiplano provides beautiful products for the home, as well as jewelry and accessories.

Experienced Goods

The best thrift store in southern Vermont. Sixty-five percent of the store's proceeds go to benefit the local hospice.

Anthropologie—www.anthropologie.com

Beyond beautiful apparel, Anthropologie also has a lovely collection of home decor items, furniture, and unique items for your home office or studio. Check out the sale bins in the home decor section for a big win!

The Container Store—www.containerstore.com

You can find solutions for all of your organization needs at this specialty retail chain. From file cabinets to carts and drawer organizers to desktop accessories, you'll find attractive ways to keep everything in place.

IKEA—www.ikea.com

A Swedish multinational group of companies that design and sell ready-to-assemble furniture, appliances, and home accessories. When furnishing your creative work space, check here for desks, storage units, chairs, shelving, and more.

Target—www.target.com

Target has really stepped up its game in home decor, making it a fab place to find affordable yet stylish items for your office or studio. Look for products designed by Oh Joy! and Emily Henderson.

West Elm—www.westelm.com

West Elm features contemporary furniture designs and housewares. If you like a modern touch, check out this store for inspiring designs and colors.

about the author

LifeSTYLE Design/Small Biz Coach, International Retreat Leader, and Founder of Sweet Spot Style, Desha Peacock is also the author of *Create the Style You Crave*. With an intuitive approach to style, Peacock's first book was listed by the *Huffington Post* as one of *The Best Books to Buy Your Girlfriend*.

As part of the Sweet Spot Style mission, Peacock works with multi-passionate female entrepreneurs to upgrade their lifeSTYLE and make money doing work they love.

Peacock holds a master's degree from The School for International Training, is a certified Global Career Development Facilitator, and has led workshops and retreats across the globe. She's been featured in *Origins Magazine*, *Design Sponge*, *Flea Market Décor Magazine*, *The Jungalow*, *Where Women Create Magazine*, *The Huffington Post*, *Career Rookie*, and *US News Money* and has made radio and TV appearances across the nation.

Desha lives in Vermont with her husband and daughter, along with Molly the dog and Clyde the cat.

You can find Desha at www.sweetspotstyle.com
or on Instagram @deshapeacock.